The RSL Market Timing System

THE RSL MARKET TIMING SYSTEM

How To Pinpoint Market Turns
—In Mutual Funds, Futures,
and Options

Humphrey E. D. Lloyd

WINDSOR BOOKS, BRIGHTWATERS, NEW YORK

Published by Windsor Books
P.O. Box 280
Brightwaters, N.Y., 11718

Manufactured in the United States of America

ISBN 0-930233-45-X

CAVEAT: It should be noted that all commodity trades, patterns, charts, systems, etc., discussed in this book are for illustrative purposes only and are not to be construed as specific advisory recommendations. Further note that no method of trading or investing is foolproof or without difficulty, and past performance is no guarantee of future performance. All ideas and material presented are entirely those of the author and do not necessarily reflect those of the publisher or bookseller.

Dedication

To Mary, My Alter Ego

Acknowledgements

I am grateful to Dow Jones-Irwin, Illinois for permission to quote from the *Encyclopedia of Technical Market Indicators* by Colby and Meyers published in 1988. ©Dow Jones-Irwin.

I am grateful also to John Wiley and Sons, 605 Third Avenue, New York, N.Y. 10158, for permission to quote from Joseph B. Stewart, Jr.'s *Dynamic Stock Option Trading*, ©1981 John Wiley and Sons, Inc. The quote is reprinted by permission.

Finally, I would like to thank my good friend, Bob Dennis, for writing the foreword. Bob is well known not only as a commodity trader, but as a commodity system designer, and it is a distinct honor for me to have him write the foreword to this book.

Table Of Contents

Figures

Tables

Foreword

My dad once said *"The only things in life that are truly worthwhile are those things that are shared with someone else."* This book is an excellent example of that. Dr. Humphrey Lloyd has been a dedicated student of the markets for over 20 years and has successfully traded the market with real money in real time for many years. He now shares with his readers everything of importance that he has learned about the market during that time.

A great many people get involved in the markets at some point in their lifetime, but a rare few become students of the market. Dr. Lloyd has spent thousands of hours analyzing hundreds of different technical indicators over the years and has developed several of his own indicators for timing market decisions. He explains in detail those indicators that have worked best for him in real time trading. For those that are technically oriented, you will recognize many of the indicators and be introduced to several new ones. The trading method that has evolved incorporates a money management technique that enters the market on a staggered basis and exists using protective stops.

Those of us who have been intimately involved for years trading the markets realize along the way that ultimate success depends on our ability to follow a disciplined approach. There are many pitfalls along the way, usually of our own making. Dr. Lloyd discusses many of these potential pitfalls and offers his experience and advice for dealing with them.

This book offers the trader a time tested, disciplined approach for trading the market. But more significantly, it emphasizes the importance of the necessary mental approach needed for successful trading.

Bob Dennis

Introduction:
The Principles Of
Successful Market Timing

In this book, I will try to present, in as concise a manner as possible, an approach to the market that has worked for me over the years in bad times as well as those much better. It is a general market timing system. I use it principally for no-load (or very low-load) mutual fund switching, but the signals are also valid for position trading in options and futures contracts. In the book's title you'll notice, *"The RSL System."* RSL stands for Relative Strength Locator. The system uses Welles Wilder's Relative Strength Index (RSI) as the locator or "point" indicator to *assess the validity* of the trading signals from the other seven indicators I use in the system. The Relative Strength Index was invented by Wilder and described in his 1978 book, *"New Concepts in Technical Trading Systems"* [1] (See Bibliography).

At the close of any trading day, the RSI will provide a number (between 0 and 100) that will enable the trader to assess where the market really is. The other timing indicators that I have come to rely on over the years will be presented and the usual RSI values at which they trigger will be discussed. The whole idea behind this system is to ensure that a sufficient number of indicators will be available, *triggering at different levels,* so that it *should* be impossible for a trader to miss being *in* for at least a good part of any significant up move or to miss being *out* for the worst part of any bad down move. Another way of expressing the idea behind this system is to say that I am trying to avoid a rigid "one-shot" approach to market timing, where everything goes when a single indicator calls for action. There are several such systems out there. I am aware that the 39-week Moving Average System (buy/sell) on the crossing is very successful when the market is moving in broad sweeps up and down and that this system has been recommended by a number of market timers. But it is a "one-shot" system and reminds me of Minnie from Trinidad. *"When she was good, she was very, very good; but when she was bad, she was awful."*

My approach divides the cash to be invested into four units (that is, each unit is 25% of the stake). There will be eight main indicators, including the RSI itself, to choose from as the market works its way up the RSI scale. But only if it *can* work its way significantly higher will all units get invested; and since each indicator will have its own exit point, the chances of taking a bad hit are greatly minimized. The name for this is money management and it is a crucial part of the system. It is certain that placing the bets in this way will not make as much money as could be made by plunking the whole wad down when the first indicator triggered *providing, and it is a very big proviso, that that indicator proved to be correct.* I have demonstrated to my own satisfaction that the approach I use will perform very satisfactorily under different market conditions; and that on a risk-adjusted basis, it is superior to an allk-or-none system. The idea is to acquire equity funds when the market is rising and to switch into money market funds when it is declining. It sounds easy, doesn't it? And it really is if you have the discipline to follow the indicators.

I have been trading the market by mutual fund switching since 1977, when telephone transfer between funds became a reality. I have been, and indeed still am, fortunate in having my retirement account with a family of funds that permits telephone switching;

16

and my experience with mutual fund switching has largely been gained by being able to use some of my retirement funds for this purpose. In 1981, I segregated a sum of money with the idea of finding out how long it would take me to double it without adding any additional funds. (The interest earned while in money market funds was, of course, counted in the total return). It took me from 9/1/81 to 1/15/85, a period of 40½ months, to double the original amount. During this time, I made 32 round-trip trades. (Positions taken as one or two units and added to were counted as one completed trade when the account was back 100% into money market funds. All the RSL indicators except the W(D)[10] and 21/5 were used). There were 26 winning trades with an average profit of 2.6%. The 6 losing trades showed an average loss of 1.1%. This is an annualized return from *real-time trading* of 29.6% and a Profit Factor of 10.24 to 1. For every $1000 lost, I showed gains of $10,240. Also, I think it is worth noting that from 10/8/82 to 4/3/84, I had a string of 15 winning trades. That is a year-and-a-half without a losing trade using this strategy! I am not a statistician, but the chances of this happening on a random basis are obviously rather small. I have not had another run of this length—mainly, I suspect, because the market is now so much more volatile. My indicators all buy strength and sell weakness. That is, for me, the only way to go.

But when trading mutual funds (except for Fidelity Selects), one can only get the *closing* price. This is a great hindrance in current markets, with huge one-day drops a reality. If the market falls out of bed without warning as it did on January 8, 1988, when it fell 140.6 Dow points, it can take back a profit present at the beginning of the day's trading and convert it into a loss. The market fell 6.9% that day and the fund that I was in fell slightly over 7%. Up until that day, I had never had to take more than a 2% loss on any one trade; but when the market fell 141 points in a day, I was forced to take almost a 3% loss on a position that I had initiated only a few trading days previously. The problem was that the decline occurred out of the clear blue sky.

17

I would accept being able only to get into a strong market on the close in mutual fund trading, if I had a chance of getting out *during the day* when my stops were hit. And that sentence contains the only flaw in the system. If I enter on a strongly up day, I get little or none of that day's action as the market will usually settle very close to the daily high; and if I exit on a strongly down day, I will have to accept the closing price, which is usually very close to the low. This was not a major problem in previous years when a big up day or down day might be 30 Dow points. However, it certainly presents a problem when the market moves 100 points or so in a single day. I have not been able to duplicate the 29.6% annualized return in mutual funds since 1985. The market has become much more volatile, so there has been more slippage of the type just discussed. And I would certainly be remiss if I were to encourage anyone to believe that such returns could be achieved with any regularity in the future if you trade only mutual funds. I think that an annual return of 12% - 18% is possible and certainly more realistic. However, as always, there are no guarantees that this or any other system will ever be profitable in the future.

I am not sure what influence program trading has had on the overall market. I am quite sure that the programs have made it considerably more difficult to succeed, but certainly not impossible to profit. This is particularly true since one of the indicators included triggers at the merest wisp of strength at a time when the market is not bursting upward. This indicator only triggers in oversold territory and is not an indicator I used back in the "old" days before all the volatility from program trading. I had observed the formation some time ago, but had not been tempted to derive an indicator that would trigger in such oversold zones as I never really had the need for one. It has become clear that with the new volatility we need an indicator to get into an upmove, if only with one unit, as early as possible. It is a great indicator and I don't think I would have been tempted to refine it if the market had continued to behave "normally." After all, for a year and a half, as I have outlined, the market came on shore for me

18

with a profit. It is tempting under such circumstances to imagine that one has found "the keys to the kingdom." This is always a dangerous feeling.

Incidentally, I have not yet paid taxes on the money that I made during that period as it is still in my retirement account making more money on a tax-deferred basis. I try to get across to my children the great advantage of tax sheltering money (via IRAs, Keoghs, 401-Ks, etc.), because what you get is freedom from the bite of taxes while the magic of compound interest goes to work. Ultimately, taxes have to be paid, of course, but on a significantly larger amount than would have accumulated without the tax-deferred benefit. The advantage is significant and the opportunity should be seized gratefully.

I know you will want to know what happened to me during the October 1987 crash. By 1987, I had acquired two unsolicited discretionary accounts (for Massachusetts friends) to trade—in addition to my own—using the no-load switch fund approach to the market. For the discretionary accounts, I moved 75% into cash on 10/6/87 and the remaining 25% out of equity funds and into cash on 10/8/87. My friends were, therefore, 100% in cash on that fateful Monday, October 19, and were happy with the situation. In my own account, I exited on October 8 with three units leaving one unit in a low-risk equity and bond fund. This, of course, is a classic case of trying to outsmart one's indicators. The indicators said *out*; indeed, I took my friends out (thank goodness). Why then was I in with one unit? Because like everyone else I had no idea that Black Monday was around the corner and leaving one unit in a balanced low-risk bond and equity fund did not seem at the time to be very risky in spite of the indicators. Fortunately, the fund held up pretty well.

I had another problem in 1987. I decided to take a longer than usual summer vacation. I do not believe in trying to monitor the market from vacationland and I want to be in cash while away (flat the market, as they say). So, I took a trading break. Unfortunately, this break occurred—as they usually do—during a big rally. So my performance in 1987 slipped for the first time below a double-digit annual percentage return and came in at a limp +6.5%. Still, I know there are investors out there who would have been quite happy with this performance.

In the market, I want to be a trader not an investor. This is primarily because I never had any identifiable stock-picking ability and, indeed, did just about everything wrong when I started. I only began gaining on the market when I concentrated on timing the market itself and forgot entirely about individual stocks. Once in awhile, I will be tempted to go for an individual stock. I have a small Keogh account and I have not managed it at all well.

My broker is a charming fellow (on the phone, as I have never met him). I am sure he would be distinctly surprised if he knew how successfully I have traded my no-load accounts, because he knows my performance with him has been mediocre at best. Whenever I buy an individual stock in my account with him, some bad news turns up about the stock soon thereafter. For instance, I bought 500 shares of a hot little Canadian stock called Grandma Lees some time ago. How could one miss with a name like that? The company was in the fast food business and produced their own fresh products like bread, soup, etc. It was trading around 11 when I bought it and it ran up to 15 or 16. I wasn't following it that carefully; but one day I couldn't find the quote and was told that trading had been halted. I never found out exactly why; but I do know that when trading resumed, the stock opened at 3, where, of course, I sold it. That is typical of my lack of success with this account.

Picking individual stocks can be extremely profitable if you have a knack for it. If you do, this market timing method can be even more critical and valuable for you. I believe that most people would be better off avoiding individual stocks altogether. After all, although it can be done, it is tough to call your broker and say, "Sell Everything." It is much easier to call your no-load fund and say, "Sell all shares of Fund X and transfer the proceeds to my money market fund." It also avoids commission costs. Of course, the argument on the other side is the Xerox

(IBM, Tampax, etc.) performance. A $1000 investment way back when and held would be worth a million dollars now. However, I know myself well enough to know that I could never hold on for that long. I am basically a trader and like to sell a stock when I think it and the market are both overbought. I accept that the really big money is not made by trading this way; but in the stock market, as in life, you have to do your own thing. I found out, some time ago, that my thing was timing the general market. I don't know how much ahead of the game I am at this point but I am convinced that I personally could never have done as well by picking individual stocks.

The ancient wisdom was to buy a good stock, put the certificate in your bottom drawer, and forget about it for a long while. That is fine if you are Will Rogers and a good stock picker. It was Will Rogers who said, after all, "Don't gamble! Take all your savings and buy some good stock and hold it until it goes up, then sell it. If it don't go up, don't buy it." (Quoted as the entry for August 11, 1989 in the *"Stock Trader's Almanac"*[2] edited by Yale Hirsch).

In the long run, it is not what you make that determines market success; it is what you keep. With my phasing-in approach to the market on the up side, I try to establish a full position if the market will let me (by acting well). But, when the tumblers turn and sell signals are in effect, I find I often reduce that position in an accelerated fashion so that at times, if several sell signals occur simultaneously, I have moved a full position out on a single trade even though that position necessitated three or four partial trades to get established.

The market is a game and a challenge. It is like a giant game of chess played on a huge board with all sorts of side games going on, and it is unfortunate that at least once in awhile you will find that one of the pieces from the game you are playing will have been snatched off the board by some arbitrary rule from the game next door that had, until that point, not concerned you at all. I believe it is possible to make money *and* have fun. Pleasure in the market for me comes from taking a signal at a time when

21

the possibility of success looks pretty slim and one's own feelings about the trade are definitely negative, and to have that trade work out *because one trusted one's indicators.*

My wife Mary is a pilot. I am not too enthusiastic about small planes, but I fly with her because I trust her judgment and I know she follows her instruments. Recently, she received her IFR (Instrument Flight Rules) rating; and for her solo instrument flight, she flew me down to Atlantic City (I needed to roll the bones) from Beverly, MA over two of the busiest TCAs (Terminal Control Areas) in the world, namely Kennedy and LaGuardia. We had a safe and successful flight. We needed her abilities to get into Bader Airport at Atlantic City and we certainly needed them on Sunday morning to get out. The fog was rolling in off the Atlantic and we couldn't see the end of the runway. I remember thinking to myself, "Should I really be doing this?" She took us up into the clouds. "Relax," I said to myself. "Mary knows what she is doing." What Mary was doing was following her indicators, in this case, her instruments. This is what anyone who wants to be successful in the market must learn to do, to let go one's personal judgment about what the market "should" do and to follow what it actually does. In effect, this comes down to a crucial philosophy, "Let your indicators make your decisions."

The real trick is to establish one's own personal way of reacting with the market. Your personal technique has two very important parameters. These are, the time frame and the vehicle used. I feel comfortable with the intermediate 3-7 week trend of the market and with no-load mutual funds. I hope to be able to describe exactly the approach I use in this book. There is no question but that someone with superior stock-picking ability has no *great* need for market timing; but even a superstar like Peter Lynch had to rethink his cash position with Magellan after the October 1987 meltdown. He was on a golfing vacation in Ireland at the time, and by all accounts had a pretty difficult time getting through to Fidelity (the vacation syndrome again). The point is—market timing can be a critical advantage for anyone, no matter what market is followed.

22

I found that my investment results improved dramatically as soon as I stopped saying to myself, "The market is due for a correction," or some such emotional and subjective assessment, and changed my thinking to, "I am going to buy now because this indicator, *which I trust,* has given a buy signal." And the signal, be it noted, had to be visible either on the chart or in a table so that, when asked by an intelligent child why I had done what I had done, I could point to the signal and identify it. As long as I can say to myself, "I did this for this good and sufficient reason," and can point to the reason, I will never blame myself if the trade does not work out. I have had some past success and hope to continue to be successful. The market, however, doesn't give a hoot what my success was in the past or however comfortable I feel with my positions.

The way I am going to describe presents a logical but certainly not the only way of playing the market, based on its position on the RSI. And here is as good a place as any to state as categorically as I can that an overbought reading on an overbought/oversold indicator is *not* an embossed invitation to short the market. Typically, a strong bull market gets overbought early on; and if it does so with authority, it will almost always work its way higher. Do not short an overbought market until you can identify that the trend of the market has indeed turned. Why am I talking about shorting the market when the switch-fund approach allows only two positions—long or cash? Well, the reason is found in the first paragraph of this introduction. *The indicators work for options and futures as well.* In fact, excellent profits are possible using this system in futures and options. And I can assure you that being short a futures position as the bull market works higher is far more uncomfortable than being on the sidelines in cash. The old market wisdom applies—be quick to turn bullish, slow to turn bearish.

We will be examining in detail indicators, including what I call specialized sub-indicators (Symbol S) which give useful additional signals when the parent indicator itself is solidly on a buy or sell. The indicators will be discussed under the following headings:

PRINCIPLE

— Why the Indicator Works and What Element of Market Action It Seeks to Isolate (There May Be More Than One)

TECHNIQUE

— Necessary Data - What Needs to Be Collected to Get Started

— Calculation — The Math Involved and Any Useful Shortcuts; Also How Long It Takes The Indicator to Stabilize

ACTION SIGNALS

— What They Are and How to Anticipate Them

STOPS

— Where to Get Out If the Indicator Fails to Act as Expected Initially

— Where to Exit a Successful Trade

SPECIALIZED SUB-INDICATORS (S)

— How They Are Used for Generating Additional Signals

OVERALL COMMENT AND SUMMARY

Chapter 1

The Relative
Strength Index (RSI)

PRINCIPLE

This superb indicator was invented by J. Welles Wilder, Jr. and described in his book, *"New Concepts in Technical Trading Systems."* [1] I believe that a better name would be, "The Relative *Internal* Strength Index," as it is the internal strength (or lack thereof) of any individual market (or stock or commodity) that is measured against itself. This is the locator indicator for the RSL System and has useful backup from my own indicator, the Moving Balance Indicator (MBI). Since the daily value of the RSI always falls between 0 and 100 (and, as we shall see, for practical purposes between 10 and 85), this indicator was chosen rather than the MBI as the locator indicator.

This indicator works by assigning market action into one of two columns—the Up Action Column and the Down Action Column. The indicator has to go up if the market goes up and vice-versa. What the indicator seeks to isolate are those times at both ends of the scale that the market is over-reacting. Because of the way the indicator is derived, the RSI value for any market has to be between 0 and 100. As the market gets oversold and falls to

25

values around 30, downside action in the market, unless the move is very strong, results in less downside movement in the RSI. The RSI is less sensitive to market change at the extremes of its range simply because of the way it is calculated. This sets up a positive divergence and the RSI may actually rise as the market falls (Fig. 1). A positive divergence is also achieved if the RSI stays flat while the market falls.

At the other end of the scale, when the market reaches RSI values around 70, a negative divergence becomes possible between the RSI and the market, with the RSI falling as the market advances (Fig. 2). A negative divergence is also achieved if the RSI stays flat as the market advances.

TECHNIQUE

Necessary Data

Wilder described in his book a 14-day RSI and we will stay with this concept, recognizing that other time frames, such as the 9-day RSI, have become popular with futures traders. Indeed, intra-day traders use the bar concept, a bar corresponding to any time period chosen from as short as one minute to a maximum of 60 minutes on an intra-day basis. It is obvious that a 14-bar RSI on, say, a 5-minute chart covers only 70 minutes of market action. But it is interesting to note that the signals generated have the same kind of validity and form the same kind of patterns as those derived from longer based daily or even weekly data. Indeed, unless the time frame is given, it is usually impossible to identify it from study of the charts alone, except when the time between bars is very short. I would stress that we are not concerned with intra-day trading in this book, so that any futures trades taken on the signals described here will be, by necessity, "position" trades.

We are going to need 14 days of market data to get going. All we are interested in is the change, on a closing basis, from one day to the next. The market can close up, down, or unchanged.

FIG. 1—RSI Positive Divergence

**Market Works
Lower**

Fail Point

Buy   RSI Sets Up
Positive Divergence

FIG. 2—RSI Negative Divergence

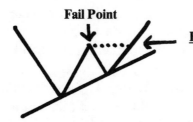

**Market Works
Higher**

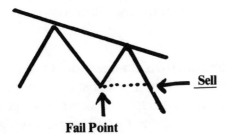

Sell   RSI Sets Up
Negative Divergence

Fail Point

These are the only possibilities. *I have always used the DJIA for calculating the RSI.* Values from the NY Comp, or S&P, will be similar but not identical. When I read Wilder's book in 1979, I had always used the New York Comp as my basic market index—and indeed I still do. I decided, however, to use the DJIA for the RSI, hoping thereby to gain some additional information. I cannot claim that doing so really profited me much as the Dow and the Comp have good positive correlation. When one goes up, the other may be expected to do so also, or at least not go down by much. (The relationship is that a move of $1.00 on the Comp is *roughly* equivalent to 16 Dow points). The fact remains, however, that the RSI in this book is based on the DJIA corrected to the first decimal place. Purists may wish to start a data base with the NY Comp or the S&P as the reference market for the RSI Index.

When the market closes exactly unchanged, no entry is made into either the up or down column. The exponential average, however, is updated for each column (see calculation). It is rare for the Dow to close exactly unchanged, although it does happen occasionally. On all other days, the change is entered into either the up column when the market is up or the down column if down. Note the change in the down column is *not* entered into the down column as a negative. A down close will increase the 14-day down column value and, therefore, decrease the RSI. There is no way a down day can cause an increase in value in the RSI, just as there is no way an up close can result in anything other than an increase in the RSI (unless the change is so small that the RSI closes unchanged). What it cannot do is close down. For the data base, we are going to need 14 days of change from the DJIA, assigning such change into up or down columns.

Calculation

Table 1 gives the up and down changes for the DJIA for the first 14 trading days in 1989. The index is started by finding the 14-day total values in both the up and down columns. These figures are divided by 14, giving the 14-day simple average value. Thereafter, the index becomes exponential, with weight being

Table 1
DATA BASE FOR RSI

1989	UP COLUMN		DOWN COLUMN
Jan 3	1	—	24.0
4	2	33.1	—
5	3	12.9	—
6	4	3.8	—
9	5	5.2	—
10	6	—	6.3
11	7	13.2	—
12	8	15.9	—
13	9	3.8	—
16	10	—	1.4
17	11	—	10.0
18	12	24.1	—
19	13	0.4	—
20	14	—	3.7
Total		112.4	45.4
÷ 14		8.03	3.24
Div.		$\dfrac{8.03}{3.24}$ +1	
=		2.48 +1	
=		3.48	
RSI (Table 2)		71	

Table 2
RELATIVE STRENGTH TABLE

$$\frac{\text{Up Column}}{\text{Down Column}} \quad + 1 \quad = \quad \text{Divisor (Div)}$$

Div	RSI	Div	RSI	Div	RSI
1.11	10	1.58	37	2.74	64
1.12	11	1.60	38	2.82	65
1.14	12	1.63	39	2.90	66
1.15	13	1.66	40	2.99	67
1.16	14	1.69	41	3.08	68
1.18	15	1.71	42	3.18	69
1.19	16	1.74	43	3.28	70
1.20	17	1.77	44	3.39	71
1.22	18	1.81	45	3.51	72
1.23	19	1.84	46	3.64	73
1.25	20	1.87	47	3.78	74
1.26	21	1.91	48	3.93	75
1.28	22	1.95	49	4.10	76
1.30	23	1.99	50	4.26	77
1.31	24	2.03	51	4.45	78
1.33	25	2.07	52	4.66	79
1.35	26	2.11	53	4.88	80
1.37	27	2.16	54	5.13	81
1.38	28	2.20	55	5.41	82
1.40	29	2.25	56	5.72	83
1.42	30	2.30	57	6.07	84
1.44	31	2.36	58	6.46	85
1.46	32	2.41	59	6.90	86
1.49	33	2.47	60	7.41	87
1.51	34	2.54	61	8.00	88
1.53	35	2.60	62	8.70	89
1.56	36	2.67	63	9.53	90

Note: To date Lowest reading 10.19.87 $\frac{11}{84}$ x
Highest reading 11.22.85

x   It has hit 83 several times in strong Bull moves. Also remember the Dow Basis.

given to the latest figure in either column. The index will take another 10 to 14 days to stabilize. (The initial 14-day base period was selected arbitrarily and clearly the 14-day up and down average figures will differ from those of other 14-day base periods that could have been chosen).

After 14 days entry into either the up or down columns, simple averages are found by totaling each column and dividing by 14. The up average is then divided by the down average. This figure *PLUS ONE* is the divisor (Div). The divisor will give the RSI directly using Table 2. Let's run the numbers for trading day 14, January 20, 1989:

The up column figure is 8.03
The down column figure is 3.24
The divisor is (8.03 divided by 3.24) + 1 = 3.48.

Using Table 2, a divisor value of 3.48 is between 3.40 = RSI 71 and 3.51 = RSI 72. The RSI is *71* (it is 71 not 72, as 3.48 is less than 3.51).

There is another way of finding the RSI. This is by expressing the up column figures as a percentage of the total of the up and down column figures, i.e.:

$$\frac{8.03}{8.03 + 3.24} \times 100 = \frac{8.03}{11.27} \times 100 \quad RSI = 71$$

Note that RSI values should always be rounded off to the nearest whole number.

By Day 14, we have derived the base index. From this point on, the averages for each column become exponential. They are very easy to calculate. If there is no entry into a column (because no change has occurred in that column), the previous day's column figure is multiplied by 13 and divided by 14, to give the new figure, which of course will always (under these circumstances) have a value lower than the previous day's value. If there is a

31

change in the column, the previous day's figure is multiplied by 13, *the day's change added* to this number and the total is then divided by 14 to give the new 14-day number. The maneuver of multiplying by 13, adding any change, and dividing by 14, results in an exponential weighting of the latest change. When calculating a *simple* moving average, it is the difference between the latest change and the change from 'x' number of periods previously that is important. This is not so in an exponential moving average. The RSI has to move in the same direction as the latest change in the market as the new up and down exponential averages are calculated using the latest change *only*.

The RSI is updated then for the rest of January 1989 as follows (Table 3). On Day 15 (January 23), the Dow fell 17.1 points. There is no entry in the up column. The previous day's value (8.03) is multiplied by 13, and divided by 14, to give the Day 15 value of 7.46:

$$8.03 \times \frac{13}{14} = 7.46$$

This is the up column value.

The 17.1 point change is entered in the down column. The previous day's figure (3.24) is multiplied by 13. 17.1 is then added to this figure and the product divided by 14:

$$
\begin{aligned}
3.24 \times 13 &= 42.12 \\
+\ 17.1 &= 59.33 \\
\div\ 14 &= 4.23
\end{aligned}
$$

This is the down column figure.

The RSI by either method is $\underline{64}$.

Method I: $\dfrac{7.46}{4.23} + 1 = 2.76 \,(\text{DIV})$

RSI $= \underline{64}\,(\text{Table 2})$

Method II: $\dfrac{7.46}{7.46 + 4.23} \times 100 = \dfrac{7.46 \times 100}{11.69} = \underline{64}$

The RSI values for the rest of January are found in similar fashion.

These are some important points to be made:

1. ↑/14 ↑ obviously means that the daily up change (if any) is followed by the 14-day up column figure. ↑/14 ↓ is just the opposite.

2. If the standard column ruled paper is used—such as National 42-383, the three columns shown in Table 3 occupy only 5 cm across (slightly less than 2 inches). These three columns hold all the necessary daily data. Since the paper has 31 vertical columns and 12 horizontal columns, almost 6 months of data can be entered and stored on a single sheet. Part of an actual worksheet is given on page 35 to show what I mean. It covers the same time period as the main table.

3. I believe it is important to condense the information into the smallest possible space from which it can be retrieved accurately. Computers are fine, but they generate reams of paper and data retrieval is dependent on an accurate filing system.

4. By the use of three columns, and Table 2, we have significantly reduced the data-base figures without losing any accuracy. Wilder used 9 columns for calculating the RSI, largely I believe to make the calculations unambiguous. But his columns can be condensed to our advantage.

5. There is a specialized sub-indicator RSI-SI buy on 1/26/89. This will be discussed shortly.

Table 3
RSI VALUES
From Jan 20 Thru Jan 30 1989
(Continuation of Table 1)

UP COLUMN ↑ /14 ↑		DOWN COLUMN ↓ /14 ↓		RSI
			Div ↓	
1.20		3.7	3.48	
	8.03		3.24	71
1.23		17.1	2.76	
	7.46		4.23	64
1.24 38.1			3.46	
	9.65		3.93	71
1.25 9.5			3.64	
	9.64		3.65	72
1.26 25.2			4.17	
	10.75		3.39	76
1.27 31.8			4.89	
	12.25		3.14	80
1.30 1.2			4.92	
	11.46		2.92	80
1.31 18.2			5.41	
	11.94		2.71	82

**Actual
Work
Sheet**

TABLE 3 (b)

1989

↑/14↑	↓/14↓	RSI
1.20 / 8.03	3.7 3.48 / 3.24	71
1.23 / 7.46	17.1 2.76 / 4.23	64
38.1 / 9.65	3.46 / 3.93	71
9.5 / 9.64	3.64 / 3.65	72
35.2 / 10.75	4.17 / 3.39	76.
31.8 / 12.25	489 / 3.4	80
1.35 / 1.2 11.46	4.92 / 2.92	80
18.2 / 11.94	5.41 / 2.71	82

ACTION SIGNALS

Wilder was concerned with divergences between the market being followed and its RSI values. If the market should make a new low, not confirmed by a new low RSI value, then a positive divergence and a failure swing became established. A buy signal occurs when the RSI takes out the intermediate peak (the fail point) in this formation (Fig. 1). On the sell side, the formation is one of negative divergence, with a sell signal occurring when the fail point is taken out (Fig. 2). Wilder stressed the importance of RSI values 30 (oversold) and 70 (overbought) in association with these divergence patterns.

As we have noted, the RSI is very popular with futures traders, and the 9-day RSI is frequently used as well as the 14-day RSI. The configurations formed by the two indicators are similar, though there is more volatility, (that is, amplitude of movement) as one would expect, in the 9-day RSI as it uses a shorter time frame. When calculating the 9-day RSI, the up and down column figures should be multiplied by 8 and divided by 9, entering the net change into up or down columns exactly as described for the 14-day RSI.

Though Wilder did not specifically recommend the use of trendline analysis for the RSI, I have found that some good signals are generated on trendline breaks. Since the RSI gives a single value for each day, trendlines will be formed. A valid down-trendline has at least three main peaks in descending order (Fig. 3). A break in such a trendline, particularly if the RSI has worked its way below 40 and crosses 40 in doing so, is a valid buy signal. The third buy signal that I have found to be effective using the RSI involves the take out to the upside of a reversal formation occurring in an upside move (Fig. 4). This signal can occur anywhere on the RSI scale. For a valid signal, I require an RSI move of at least 4 points against the primary trend.

Buy signals occur then:

1. On positive divergence (Fig. 1)
2. On a trendline break—particularly if in doing so, the index crosses RSI 40 (Fig. 3)
3. Any time a reversal point is taken out (Fig. 4)

Using the switch-fund approach, when a one-time during the day decision is all that is required, it is easy to use the market number from, say, 15 minutes before the close in the RSI formula to see if that would generate a signal. When the market is strong, the signal will usually be clear-cut. If, however, the signal is "on the line," it may mean waiting a day before making the trade in order to find out exactly where the market closed. Funny things happen just before the close, particularly on days when options and futures contracts expire.

FIG. 3— RSI Trendline Break

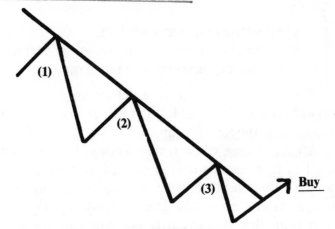

FIG. 4—RSI Reversal Buy Signal

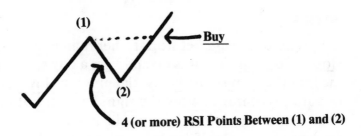

4 (or more) RSI Points Between (1) and (2)

FIG. 5—RSI Reversal Sell Signal

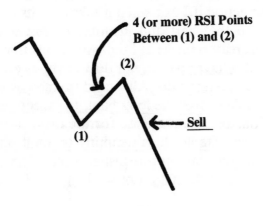

4 (or more) RSI Points Between (1) and (2)

Sell signals are just the opposite of those described as buy signals:

1. On negative divergence (Fig. 2)
2. On a trendline break (see discussion in next section)
3. Any time a reversal point is taken out (Fig. 5)

These are then the buy and sell action signals using the RSI as an indicator on its own. But the RSI is also used as the "locator" indicator in the RSL system.

After the close of each market day, it is essential to calculate the RSI to assess the overall strength or weakness of the market, as the other indicators we will be describing characteristically trigger at different RSI levels. Knowing the RSI value is an important first step towards assessing the validity of the signals that will be generated.

STOPS

I prefer to use market stops rather than money management stops. If the market turns up and I get a buy signal, it is clear to me that the stop is just below the previous low. This will be a certain percentage below the signal point, but it won't be a fixed percentage below it, nor will it represent a fixed dollar amount of loss. But if the market takes out the reversal low, it will have given me some vital information, namely that it will try to head lower. It may fake me out, of course, take out the low (on a *closing* basis) and then reverse to the upside. But I will have a *solid* reason for action if I exit when it takes out its reversal low, as I can point to the chart and identify, *by the action of the market itself,* the reason for what I did. And really that is all I can require of myself. I have no idea, nor does anybody else, what the market is actually going to do. All I need to know is why I took the action I did. And over the long haul, the successes with this approach will more than make up for the inevitable failures. And I do mean inevitable. It is tempting to want all trades to work out; tempting, but not realistic. I have absolutely no patience now with a trade that is not working out. I boot it out as soon as the market tells me that the original signal has failed. Over the years, I have managed to develop a ruthlessness that surprises the old haphazard investor that I used to be, when hope and pray ruled my investment day. I am now very good at cutting my losses. But I still have some work to do on letting my profits run. Part of the problem here is related to the fact that the sell signals from the indicators I use are not as clear-cut as the buy signals. This is at least partly because the market usually takes longer to top out than it does to bottom out. But I must also admit that part of the problem relates to a desire I can recognize in myself of wanting to nail down profits. But here again, I will not blame myself for an exit that proves to be premature as long as I can identify a valid reason for my action.

So far, I realize this has been a general discussion about stops rather than those specific for the RSI. Actually, when trading the no-load mutual funds via switching, it is not possible to enter a stop *as a stop*. But it is essential to know exactly where you want to get out of a trade. This is why a *close* below a previous low (for a long trade or *above* a previous high if short in futures and options) is the best stop of all. Using the RSI entry rules, the stop is easy to identify and the actual market level that would give such an RSI reading is readily found by plugging in some hypothetical numbers into the previous day's values. Fig. 6 gives the RSI stop following a buy. Note that point 4, if it forms, is the action point, not point 2. If, however, point 2 is taken out immediately, it becomes the stop point. There is only one problem using this formation as a stop. The market will usually have to move quite significantly against the trade to trigger it.

A stop then is basically a protective device. Early on in the trade, it is designed to protect against significant loss. But what should be done when the trade develops a profit? Where is the exit point? Using the RSI, I have noticed that a break in an uptrend line tends to give premature signals. One way around this is to use what I call the fail-safe line. I came up with this concept in the fall of 1982 when I was looking for a method that would have kept me in that incredible move which started in August

FIG. 6—RSI Sell Stop

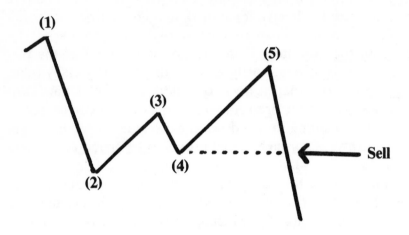

1982 through the September correction. I re-entered in October, but I would have done better by staying in with at least a unit or two. What I came up with was the thrust concept. I found that if a best-fit angle for the thrust of the initial move was drawn through the move, then an angle one-third less than this angle would have done the trick. Those familiar with Edson Gould's speed resistance lines will recognize the similarity, the difference being that the thrust angle is drawn through the move.

At any rate, if the angle of a valid RSI regular uptrend line is found, (and the actual angle will, of course, vary with the scale used), then a fail-safe line at two-thirds of this angle often works surprisingly well. When crossed, it will usually—though not always—give a better exit price than that from the penetration of the original uptrend line itself. Fig. 7 illustrates this concept during the late 1985 market. The trick is to stay in for as long as possible without giving too much back. If you wait for weakness, as I believe you should, it is inevitable that some potential profit will not be realized. This should be thought of as the cost of doing business.

My indicators basically buy strength and sell weakness. I have never found a way—and I do not believe there is one—to buy weakness when weakness is *all* there is to go on. The RSI for Friday, October 16, 1987 closed at a value of 22. This was (and is) in highly oversold territory, but it is absolutely *not* an invitation to buy just because of this (as Black Monday, October 19, demonstrated beyond any doubt). It is essential to wait for the market to give some indication that it has turned before buying, no matter how oversold an oscillator reading gets. There is no exception that I know of to this rule. The same is basically true on the sell side. Don't sell, and particularly don't sell short, just because the market is overbought and appears too high. But whereas there is no way that I know of to go fishing for a bottom successfully, there are two formations that we will be discussing, one under the MBI and the other under the envelope indicators, that have been quite successful at picking tops.

Specialized Sub-Indicators (Symbol S)

There are two RSI specialized sub-indicators:

1. RSI - S I
   A move above RSI 70 to RSI 74 for a *BUY*
2. RSI - S II
   A move below RSI 30 to RSI 28 for a *SELL*

Wilder looked on RSI values of 70 and 30 as reversal areas in overbought and oversold market conditions, respectively. Most of the time this holds true, but from time to time, the market will develop such internal momentum that it will thrust through the RSI 70 value. If it can reach an RSI value of 74, I have found that it will usually work its way higher over the next few weeks or even longer. Table 4 gives the details of the 11 times this has happened since 1980, using RSI 74 as a buy signal and holding the position (ignoring any similar repeat buy formations) until the RSI has fallen to 50. RSI 50 was chosen somewhat arbitrarily as a figure at which the initial momentum could safely be assumed to have dissipated. A total of 742 Dow points would have been gained in 11 trades, of which 8 were winners. The average loss for the three

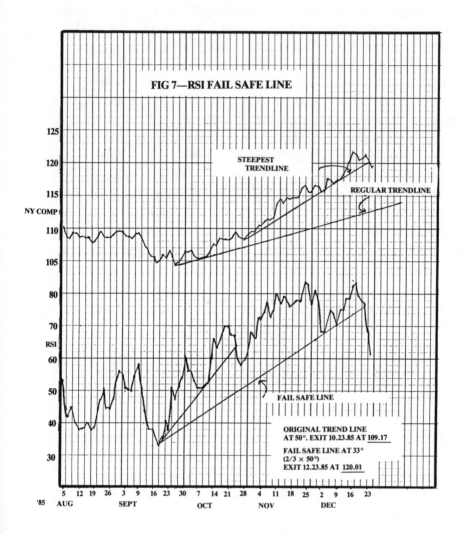

FIG 7—RSI FAIL SAFE LINE

STEEPEST
TRENDLINE

REGULAR TRENDLINE

NY COMP

RSI

FAIL SAFE LINE

ORIGINAL TREND LINE
AT 50°. EXIT 10.23.85 AT 109.17

FAIL SAFE LINE AT 33°
(2/3 × 50°)
EXIT 12.23.85 AT 120.01

'85 AUG   SEPT   OCT   NOV   DEC

losing trades was 9.4 points. The average of all trades was a gain of 67.5 points.

The important point to realize, of course, is that we were for most of the time in a roaring bull market. These figures certainly underscore the folly of shorting a bull market just because it is overbought. It takes a good deal of courage to buy under these conditions, but it is clearly the correct thing to do, and it is a terrific feeling to have the trade work out. The first time I bought an upside break-out in clearly overbought territory, I felt terribly uncomfortable and had mentally to lecture myself to get the trade off. But it worked out beautifully.

Similarly, a move below 30 that can carry to 28 or below (a slightly greater move on a percentage basis than that from 70 to 74 on RSI - SI) is a sell, that is a *sell short*, signal (RSI - S II). Since we were in a strong bull market during most of the period from 1980 to the present (1/90), we would not expect as many sell signals as there were RSI - S I buy signals nor were there. Table 5 gives the sell short signals (RSI 28) using a value of RSI 40 as the Buy (cover) signal. Short selling is not really very well understood by those not actively engaged in the practice, but all that is involved is a reversal of the normal buy now, sell later sequence. A trader sells short, thereby establishing the *sale* price hoping to buy in the short position—cover it—later at a profit when the security held short will hopefully have declined in value. It is as simple as that.

There were five trades, 4 winners and 1 loser. The winner's batting average was greatly helped by the October 1987 freefall, but the other three winning trades showed an average gain of 50.2 points without the October figure. The 4 winning trades with the October 1987 figure gained an average of 122.9 points, as opposed to the single loss of 8.2 points. The average of all trades was a gain of 96.7 points.

Mutual funds as a general rule cannot be shorted (we will discuss those that can be later), but options and futures offer opportunities on the short side. It is important to explore the possibilities that exist on the short side of the market once a

Table 4
RSI - S I

DATE	BUY RSI 74 DJIA	DATE	SELL RSI 50 DJIA	GAIN (LOSS)
1. 6/ 4/80	858.0	7/15/80	901.5	+ 43.5
2. 8/20/82	869.3	9/29/82	906.3	+ 37.0
3. 10/ 7/82	966.0	11/16/82	1008.0	+ 42.0
4. 4/28/83	1219.5	5/18/83	1203.6	(− 15.9)
5. 8/ 3/84	1202.1	9/10/84	1202.5	+ 0.4
6. 1/23/85	1274.7	3/ 8/85	1269.7	(− 5.0)
7. 11/ 5/85	1396.7	1/ 9/86	1518.2	+ 121.5
8. 2/ 7/86	1613.4	4/ 4/86	1739.2	+ 125.8
9. 1/14/87	2035.0	3/30/87	2278.4	+ 243.4
10. 6/22/87	2445.5	9/ 2/87	2602.0	+ 156.5
11. 1/26/89	2291.1	2/22/89	2283.9	(− 7.2)

Total Dow Points Gained
= 742.0
Average Gain Per Trade
= 67.5 Dow Points

Table 5
RSI - S II

DATE	SELL SHORT RSI 28 DJIA	DATE	BUY (Cover) RSI 40 DJIA	GAIN (LOSS)
8/24/81	900.1	9/29/81	847.9	+ 52.2
6/ 4/82	805.0	6/23/82	813.2	(− 8.2)
2/ 1/84	1212.3	3/23/84	1154.8	+ 57.4
5/ 4/84	1165.3	6/ 1/84	1124.4	+ 40.9
10/15/87	2355.1	11/ 2/87	2014.1	+ 341.0

Total Dow Points Gained
= 483.3
Average Gain Per Trade
= 96.7 Dow Points

degree of familiarity with all the indicators making up the RSL System has been acquired.

OVERALL COMMENT AND SUMMARY

There is no doubt that the RSI was a major invention and Wilder is to be congratulated for discovering it. It has a beautiful internal logic about it. The values *have* to fall between 0 and 100. In my records of the RSI based on the Dow, 11 and 84 (11/22/85) are the extreme readings to date. The RSI closed at 11 on 10/19/87. Even if the Dow had fallen another 100 points the following day (and I am not the only person glad that it did not), the RSI would only have fallen to 10. On the upside, I think it is quite unlikely that a value of 85 will be exceeded.

What happens is that, as the indicator moves towards either extreme, it runs out of space so to speak, making divergences occur. But it must again be emphasized that a negative divergence in a bull market, particularly the first negative divergence, is not an indication to sell and particularly it is not an invitation to sell short. A positive divergence in oversold territory on the other hand is more reliable and is usually a valid buy signal. The stock market has a definite upward bias, partly because the average player is optimistic and prefers to be a buyer rather than a seller. Of course, being an optimist in a true bear market won't do a thing for you. That is when the short sellers clean up. Some traders indeed have a strong bearish bias and do most of their trading from the short side. But they get mangled when the bull kicks up its heels, which it can do without warning. When the bull is off and running it is important to stay with the beast as long as possible. RSI - S I will alert you to the momentum underlying the market. This is the time to get the last dollar down if it is not already down.

And when the market is falling out of bed, RSI - S II will warn you not to go bottom fishing. RSI - S II had already flashed a sell signal on *Thursday*, October 15, 1987 with a reading of 28. Buying a couple of OEX puts or shorting a futures contract on the S&P or NYFE at Thursday's close would have yielded some fantastic profits a few trading days later. On the other hand, sellers of puts, those who had been smiling all the way to the bank during the big bull market, saw their world explode in front of their eyes, losing not only all their laboriously acquired profits but often (if defensive action was not in place) entering the harrowing world of staggering margin calls and unbelievable losses.

One of the beauties of Wilder's RSI is that it can be used to compare one market with another. For instance, although I no longer trade in this fashion, I had a successful trading period spreading the S&P futures against the Value Line futures. All I did was run a 9-day RSI on both contracts. I then expressed the 9-day RSI S&P divided by the 9-day RSI Value Line as a percentage. Using a crossing of the 100% line, I would buy the stronger, sell the weaker contract. Straightforward trendline analysis also gave some good signals. Although I was quite successful, I realized that I was more interested in timing the market itself than I was in trying to make sense of the differing behavior between the two contracts. Actually, now I come to think of it, a market timer is not trying to make sense of the market. The task is to catch a market turn early enough to profit from it. I think the real reason I no longer trade spreads is that the signals tend to "whip" more than regular market timing signals. But once a trend gets established, a spread can be a very satisfactory way to trade such volatile markets. If you decide to give it a shot, I recommend plotting the net difference between the cash indices on a daily basis in addition to plotting the 9 day RSI percent ratio on the futures contracts.

In 1988, Colby and Meyers book, *"The Encyclopedia of Technical Market Indicators,"*[3] was published. One of the indicators they discussed was the RSI. They have this to say:

"Despite its name, it has absolutely nothing in common with the traditional relative strength concept, whereby the price of a stock is divided by a broad market index (such as the Standard and Poor's 500 Index) to arrive at a ratio that shows the trend of a stock's performance relative to the general market." Page 433.

I have waited to bring up this aspect, since it is made well by

Colby and Meyers. As they point out, relative strength traditionally was assessed by comparing the action of an individual stock to a broad market index, whereas as I noted in the section under Principle, the RSI is an *internal* relative strength index of any individual market.

Colby and Meyers further state:

"In numerous trial runs of various combinations, the best and least ambiguous decision rule for interpreting RSI we found was to buy when RSI rises above 50, and sell and sell short when RSI falls below 50." Page 435. The optimization runs they showed illustrated that the 21 *week* RSI was the most successful. It should be noted that all their indicators have a longer time frame than the ones I use, their reference indicator being a simple 40-week moving average cross-over.

In a later chapter, I will give details of the RSI levels at which the other indicators of the RSL System may be expected to kick in and how to use this information. In this summary of the RSI itself, I would like to re-emphasize the philosophy of the RSL System. Originally, I though of calling it the "Relative Strength System," but decided against doing so because the other indicators involved, and they are all important, are based on several different concepts. The whole idea behind the RSL System is one of getting at least a good piece of the action from any up move in the market, and doing so by adding progressively to the position if the market action warrants such a decision. The RSI is the locator indicator for the other indicators, hence the title, *"RSL System"—Relative Strength Locator System.* But the other indicators are individually important in deciding upon trading action both for entering the market on the upside and for exit points after the market turns to the downside. The first order of business, then, before the opening of any new trading day is to calculate the 14-day RSI based on the Dow Jones Industrial Average. The next order of business is to calculate the Moving Balance Indicator (MBI).

Chapter 2

The Moving Balance
Indicator (MBI)

PRINCIPLE

I started work on trying to find my own "definitive" indicator on January 1, 1973 after reading Larry Williams' book, *"The Secret of Selecting Stocks For Immediate and Substantial Gains."* [4] This book was a complete revelation to me, as I had no idea until I read it that anything like technical analysis existed. All I knew was that I was no good at investing. That annoyed me as I had managed to achieve an acceptable degree of competence and success at everything else I had tried. It took me over two years and a good deal of work, both historical and in real-time, but finally I found an indicator that seemed to work pretty well. How I isolated the components and put them together was fully detailed in my book, *"The Moving Balance System, A New Technique for Stock and Option Trading."* [5] The indicator I called the Moving Balance Indicator or MBI.

My idea was to try to find an indicator that would identify extremes in overbought and oversold areas, hoping that these extremes would, like an overstretched spring, cause trend reversal. I introduced a zone concept and I felt that once the market got sufficiently overbought or oversold, it would internally *and of itself* correct the condition. During 1973 and 1974, and also on historical analysis going back for several years, that is the way the market seemed to work most of the time; indeed, with a sufficient degree of accuracy for me to want to record my observations.

The indicator I came up with had three individual components. I was hoping to isolate the big wave moves, as I felt the market could not get significantly overbought or oversold without a sizable contribution from *each* of the three components. I have never then or now been able to make volume work well for me on its own; but I decided to have as one of the components the 10 day moving average of the up volume of the issues traded on the Big Board. I ignored the down volume entirely in this component, believing that by doing so I would be able to isolate overbought areas more accurately. I was not so worried about identifying oversold areas as the other two components did a fine job of that.

The three components were: (1) **The A-D Component:** This was derived from the 10 day moving average (MA) of the advancing issues divided by the 10 day moving average of the declining issues. This figure was multiplied by ten. (2) **The Advancing Volume Component:** This was derived from the 10 day MA of the advancing volume. The original figures were entered with three zeros dropped and the final figure was divided by a thousand. This meant that a 10 day moving average of advancing volume with a value of 20,572 represented 20.572 million shares of advancing volume and entered the MBI at this value rounded off to the second place of decimals, i.e., as 20.57. (3) **The Traders' Index Component (TRIN):** The Traders' Index was invented by Richard Arms and is also known as the Arms Index. I came to refer to it as the MKDS Component; its symbol on the Bunker-Ramo Quote Machine, although it is much more commonly now referred to as TRIN (**Tr**aders **In**dex). I will update my thinking and refer to it as TRIN in this book even though I used MKDS throughout the original Moving Balance System book. TRIN is a reciprocal indicator. Values below 1.00 are bullish and become increasingly so as the value decreases.

Values above 1.00 are bearish and become increasingly so as the value increases. Obviously such values cannot be used directly as a component of the MBI, so I assigned values to the TRIN, reversing its reciprocality. A 10 day moving average TRIN reading of 1.00 was assigned a value of 6.0; and for each 0.05 in the average that the TRIN decreased relative to 1.0, the assigned value increased by 0.5. A 10 day moving average TRIN of 0.9 was assigned a value of 7.0. On the other side of unity, the assigned value decreased as the TRIN increased. A 10 day moving average TRIN value of 1.1 was assigned a value of 5.0.

(4) The MBI itself was calculated by taking the product of the three components, multiplying by two, and rounding off to the nearest whole number.

So far, so good. Figure 8 shows how the MBI performed in 1974 relative to the New York Comp. What I was trying to do was buy at the bottom and sell at the top, not realizing then that this cannot be done. But I did have a good deal of success in 1974 selling naked options at MBI highs, principally because we were in a bear market; and in a bear market, the market itself and the MBI will usually reverse within a day or two of each other.

Fortunately for my understanding of the overall market, the 1975 bull market came along. It made me realize that in bull markets, the MBI gets overbought early on and previously successful sell signals taken at what were MBI highs in a bear market were no longer profitable; indeed, just the reverse.

As I mentioned, one component, the 10 day moving average of the advancing volume, was on its own. Only four elements are used in calculating the MBI: (1) Advancing issues (2) Declining Issues (3) Advancing volume and (4) Declining volume. By allowing the advancing volume additional weight, I hoped to be able to differentiate really strong moves from those not so strong; but what I have failed to allow for was any significant increase in total volume.

In 1974, the greatest 10 day MA figure of the advancing volume was, believe it or not, 10.85 on January 4, 1974. This, of

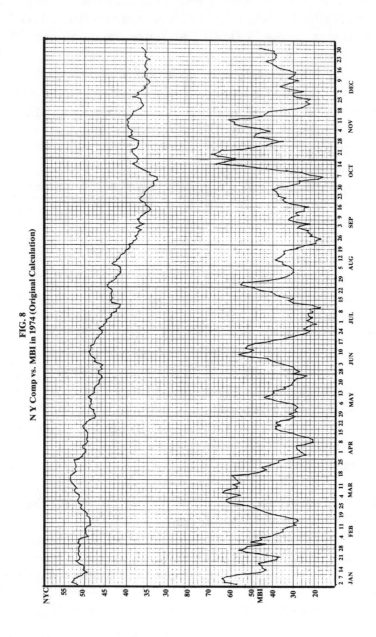

FIG. 8
N Y Comp vs. MBI in 1974 (Original Calculation)

52

course, equals a 10-day advancing volume MA of 10.85 million shares. By 1987, the 10-day MA of the advancing volume hit a value of 130.36 (that is, 130.36 million shares on January 16, 1987, 12 times the 1974 figure).

It became obvious to me, of course, long before 1987 that there was a problem and I wrote an update in 1983 suggesting two ways of attacking this problem. These modifications work quite well. The suggestions were: (1) Use semi-log paper to reduce the amplitude of the MBI and (2) to apply a volume correction factor to the advancing volume component. But what really blew the old way of calculating the indicator out of the water was the small correction, a.k.a. the Crash of 1987. It was the TRIN component that unraveled, as will be discussed.

The new method of calculating the MBI volume-proofs the indicator. Since the patterns obtained from both methods of calculation are comparable, I have decided just to keep calling the indicator the MBI and not to use a modifier, such as new MBI or MBI II. All MBI values in this book were obtained by the *new* method of calculation unless otherwise indicated. I hope this is not a confusion for those used to the old method. In the new method of calculating the MBI, the A/D component is unchanged. The TRIN component now has different assigned values but is otherwise unchanged. The real difference is in the advancing volume component. The advancing volume is now expressed as a percentage of the total advancing and declining volume (ignoring any unchanged volume). A 10-day MA is *then* run on these percentages *and the figure obtained divided by three.*

Obviously, the percentage figure can never be greater than 100 or less than 0. In practice, the 10-day MA figures will vary between 35 and 65 most of the time. This maneuver volume-proofs the MBI and also isolates the true significance of the advancing volume component; the contribution that the advancing volume makes to the total active volume. Remember that the 10-day MA figures are divided by three in calculating the MBI.

TECHNIQUE

Necessary Data:
The following data must be collected on a daily basis:
1. The number of advancing issues;
2. The number of declining issues;
3. Advancing volume;
4. Declining volume;
Since the indicators are based on 10-day MA's, there is no stabilization period.

Calculation:
1. **The A/D Component:** Run a 10-day MA of the advancing issues. Divide this by a 10-day MA of declining issues and multiply by 10. Table 6 shows how to set up this component using the daily figures of January '89. In Table 6, on the new Day 1 (January 17), 624 issues advanced as opposed to 619 issues on the old Day 1 (January 3). The new 10-day MA is obtained by adding 1/10 of the difference to the old MA value to give the new MA value; i.e., $\frac{624 - 619}{10}$ + 836.8 = 837.3. Attention has to be paid to enter the new day first, subtracting the old day. For instance, on new Day 4 (January 20), 659 issues advanced compared to old Day 4 (January 6) advances of 964. The previous day's moving average was 819.9. The new moving average is $\frac{659 - 964}{10}$ + 819.9 = 789.4. The 10-day MA of the declining issues is found in identical fashion. The A/D Component on January 16 was $\frac{836.8}{634.7}$ × 10 = 13.2.
2. **The Advancing Volume Component:** Calculate for each day the percentage that the advancing volume is of the total active volume (that is, the advancing volume plus declining volume). Do *not* use the unchanged volume values. Run a 10-day MA of the daily percentage

readings and divide these values by three, rounding off to the first place of decimals (Table 7).

3. **The TRIN Component:** TRIN is calculated on a daily basis as follows: TRIN = the number of advancing issues, divided by the number of declining issues, multiplied by the declining volume, divided by the advancing volume. The 10-day MA is run (Table 8). This figure corrected to the first decimal place is then given its assigned value using Table 9.

4. **The MBI:** Add the three components together, multiply by 1.5, and round off to the nearest total number. The 1.5 factor is used rather than the original 2 factor, as the 1.5 factor makes the MBI values comparable to RSI values.

You will remember that I advised (when discussing the RSI) keeping the data in as small a space as possible consistent with accurate retrieval. I hope you are ready for this as Table 10 gives a copy of my actual MBI worksheet for the period in question. There are several points:

1. The 10-day MA figures are to be found *above* the daily advancing and declining figures.
2. The total of advancing volume and declining volume is above the declining volume figure.
3. The 10-day MA of the TRIN is above the daily figure.
4. The check marks at the end of each week mean that the 10-day MA mathematics have been verified.
5. The three values for calculating the MBI are identified by an arrowed circle.

This Table will give you an idea of the amount of information that can be stored on a single sheet. I do not believe in trying to fill every block as this leads to eye fatigue and mistakes. Go over the figures for January carefully. You will recognize all of them from Tables 6, 7, 8 and 9. I believe that keeping careful, neat, and legible data is a top priority, and keeping them up to date is

Table 6
MBI A/D COMPONENT
A = 10-Day MA Adv. iss.

D = 10-Day MA Decl iss.

1989	ADV. ISS.	10-DAY MA	DECL. ISS.	10-DAY MA	A/D ×10
JAN 3	¹ 619		942		
4	² 1187		ʼ331		
5	³ 837		611		
6	⁴ 964		522		
7	⁵ 860		639		
10	⁶ 621		816		
11	⁷ 822		606		
12	⁸ 907		586		
13	⁹ 836		615		
16	¹⁰ 695	836.8	679	634.7	13.2
17	¹ 624	837.3	800	620.5	13.5
18	² 1036	822.2	474	634.8	13.0
19	³ 814	819.9	643	638.0	12.9
20	⁴ 659	789.4	755	661.3	11.5
23	⁵ 553	756.7	912	658.6	11.0
24	⁶ 1009	795.5	477	654.7	12.2
25	⁷ 820	795.3	648	658.9	12.1
26	⁸ 962	800.8	510	651.3	12.3
27	⁹ 929	810.1	611	650.9	12.4
30	¹⁰ 876	828.2	570	640.0	12.9
31	¹ 960	861.8	541	614.1	14.0

56

Table 7
MBI ADV. VOL. COMPONENT

1989		↑ VOL.	↓ VOL.	TOTAL ↑+↓	% ↑	10-DAY MA	÷3
1. 3	1	29820	85470	115290	26		
4	2	123330	12420	135750	91		
5	3	95410	51930	147340	65		
6	4	99900	41850	141750	70		
9	5	72750	69070	141820	51		
10	6	53190	59360	112550	47		
11	7	88000	35010	123010	72		
12	8	106970	49190	156160	69		
13	9	66950	38150	105100	64		
16	10	55930	39050	94980	59	61.4	20.5
17	1	60120	61270	121390	50	63.8	21.3
18	2	131150	32560	163710	80	62.7	20.9
19	3	100860	71630	172430	58	62.0	20.7
20	4	76690	67500	144190	53	60.3	20.1
23	5	22090	88590	110680	20	57.2	19.1
24	6	136310	33320	169630	80	60.5	20.2
25	7	105420	54910	160330	66	59.9	20.0
26	8	143950	46380	190330	76	60.6	20.2
27	9	175910	58470	234380	75	61.7	20.6
30	10	101000	47820	148820	68	62.6	20.9
31	1	130930	39580	170510	77	65.3	21.8

Table 8
MBI TRIN COMPONENT

DATE	TRIN	10-DAY MA	ASSGN'D VALUE
JAN 3	1 1.88		
4	2 0.36		
5	3 0.75		
6	4 0.77		
9	5 1.31		
10	6 0.85		
11	7 0.54		
12	8 0.71		
13	9 0.77		
16	10 0.71	0.865	11.0
17	1 0.79	0.756	11.5
18	2 0.54	0.774	11.5
19	3 0.90	0.789	11.5
20	4 0.77	0.789	11.5
23	5 2.43	0.901	11.0
24	6 0.52	0.868	11.0
25	7 0.66	0.880	11.0
26	8 0.61	0.870	11.0
27	9 0.51	0.844	11.5
30	10 0.73	0.846	11.5
31	1 0.55	0.822	11.5

Table 9
MBI TRIN ASSIGNED VALUE

10-DAY MA TRIN	ASSGN'D VALUE		10-DAY MA TRIN	ASSGN'D VALUE
0.6	12.5		2.4	3.5
0.7	12.0		2.5	3.0
0.8	11.5		2.6	2.5
0.9	11.0		2.7	2.0
1.0	10.5		2.8	1.5
1.1	10.0		2.9	1.0
1.2	9.5		3.0	0.5
1.3	9.0		3.1	0
1.4	8.5		3.2	−0.5
1.5	8.0		3.3	−1.0
1.6	7.5		3.4	−1.5
1.7	7.0		3.5	−2.0
1.8	6.5		3.6	−2.5
1.9	6.0		3.7	−3.0
2.0	5.5		3.8	−3.5
2.1	5.0		3.9	−4.0
2.2	4.5		4.0	−4.5
2.3	4.0			

Table 10
MBI WORKSHEET

1989	10-DAY MA ADV.	10-DAY MA DECL.	A/D ×10	↑VOL.	Tot.Vol. ↓VOL.	%↑/T	10-DAY MA	+3	10-DAY MA TRIN	ASS. VAL.	MBI
1.3	762.0 / 619	641.3 / 942	11.0	29820	115290 / 85470	26	55.6	18.5	0.975 / 1.88	10.5	60
	746.6 / 1187	664.6 / 321	12.0	123230	125750	91	57.0	19.0	0.970 / 0.36	10.5	62
	815.1 / 837	641.2 / 611	12.8	95410	147340 / 51930	65	59.7	19.9	0.968 / 0.75	10.5	65
	845.6 / 964	618.6 / 522	12.8	99900	141780 / 41880	70	61.5	20.5	0.920 / 0.77	11.0	68
1.9	7614 / 860	601.1 / 639	14.3	72750	141820 / 69070	51	61.6	20.5	0.955 / 1.31	10.5	68
	838.4 / 621	633.9 / 816	13.2	53190	112550 / 59360	47	58.4	19.5	0.993 / 0.85	10.5	65
	865.2 / 822	614.5 / 606	14.1	88000	123010 / 35010	72	61.4	20.5	0.951 / 0.54	10.5	68
	876.9 / 957	611.9 / 585	14.3	106970	158160 / 41140	69	62.0	20.7	0.944 / 0.71	11.0	69
	841.8 / 993	626.2 / 615	13.8	66950	105100 / 38150	64	60.2	26.1	0.977 / 0.77	10.5	67
1.16	836.8 / 695	634.7 / 679	13.2	55930	114960 / 39050	59	61.4	20.5	0.865 / 0.71	11.0	67

Table 10 (Cont'd)
MBI WORKSHEET

1989	10-DAY MA ADV.	10-DAY MA DECL.	A/D X10	↑VOL.	TOT.VOL. ↓VOL.	%↑ T	10-DAY MA	+3	10-DAY MA TRIN	ASS. VAL.	MBI
1	5373.3 / 624	6205 / 800	13.5	60120	121340 / 61270	50	63.8	21.3	0.756 / 0.79	11.5	69
2	5222 / 1036	6248 / 474	-13.0	131150	162710 / 31560	80	61.7	20.9	0.774 / 0.54	11.5	68
3	5144 / 814	6380 / 643	12.9	100800	172430 / 71630	58	62.0	20.7	0.789 / 0.90	11.5	68
+	7694 / 659	6613 / 755	11.7	76690	144940 / 67500	53	60.3	20.1	0.789 / 0.77	11.5	65
5 (1.23)	7756.7 / 553	6686.6 / 912	11.0	22090	110660 / 86540	20	57.2	19.1	10.901 / 2.43	11.0	62
6	7455 / 1009	6547 / 477	12.2	136310	169630 / 38520	65	60.5	20.2	0.883 / 0.52	11.0	65
7	7455.3 / 820	6589 / 648	12.1	105420	160330 / 54410	66	59.9	20.0	0.880 / 0.66	11.0	65
8	7406.8 / 962	651.3 / 510	12.3	143950	190330 / 46350	76	60.6	20.2	0.870 / 0.61	11.0	65
9	7401 / 729	650.9 / 611	12.4	175910	237350 / 58470	75	61.7	20.6	0.844 / 0.51	11.5	67
10 (1.30)	7262.2 / 8768	16400.0 / 570	12.9	101000	148220 / 47320	89	62.6	20.9	0.846 / 0.73	11.5	68
1	7361.8 / 960	614.1 / 541	14.0	136930	170510 / 34560	77	65.3	21.8	0.830 / 0.55	11.5	71

61

essential for success. This is not a game one can play in a haphazard fashion. I believe that a commitment to keeping good records must be made; and if the task seems too onerous and time-demanding, then that will be a valuable piece of information to have before one decides to get started.

I also believe in updating charts manually even though a computer may be available. I am convinced a better feel for the market is acquired by doing so. Furthermore, I believe it is easier to retrieve data from manual work sheets than from computer storage.

The RSL System requires about 30-45 minutes a day for daily posting and another hour or two on the weekend to check the math, update any weekly data, and for planning. This makes a total time commitment of about 5 hours a week to the system, once the initial work sheets have been drawn up and the initial data organized.

ACTION SIGNALS

Originally, I had hoped it would be possible to take action when the MBI got significantly overbought or oversold. But, as with the RSI, significantly overbought or oversold readings are not, *in themselves*, invitations to bet on a market reversal. In a bull market, the MBI will very characteristically top-out early, that is before the market, and may indeed do so in a good rally in a bear market, although not characteristically. What should be looked for? Figs. 9 and 10 give the MBI values for 1987 and 1988, respectively. The scale had to be kept small, so the charts appear less sensitive than they actually are. 1987 was a particularly instructive year, as it showed extreme readings at both ends of the scale. The January reading of 90 was as overbought as it gets. The

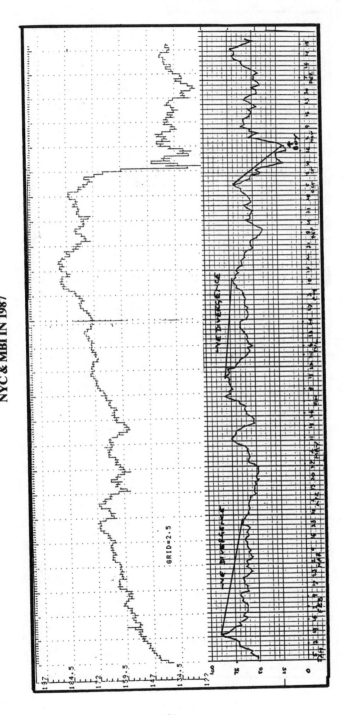

Fig. 9
NYC & MBI IN 1987

GRID=2.5

-VE DIVERGENCE

-VE DIVERGENCE

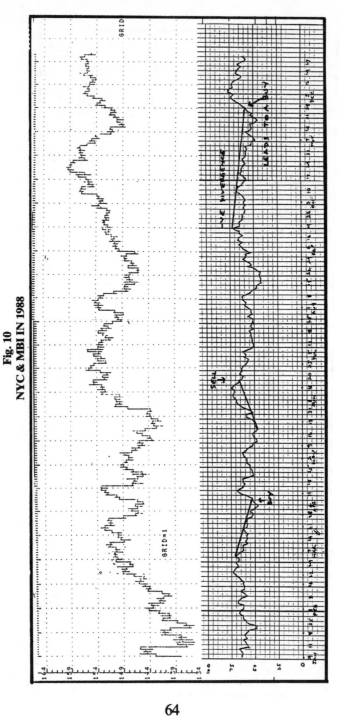

Fig. 10
NYC & MBI IN 1988

October reading of 15 on 10/26 and 10/27/87 was as oversold as the MBI has ever been.

Most of the time, however, as can be seen in 1988, the MBI fluctuates between values of 45 and 70. A value below 45 is oversold and one above 70 is overbought. While these values are similar to the RSI values, it is clear that the MBI becomes oversold at a somewhat higher value than the RSI. The range from 45-70 does not seem very large, but it takes a good market move to advance the MBI from oversold to overbought levels.

The trend is deemed to have reversed when MBI 45 is crossed from below to above. In overbought territory, when MBI 70 is the overbought value, a return to a value below 70 is not of itself a sell signal because of the tendency of the MBI to top-out ahead of the market.

One of the characteristics of overbought-oversold oscillators is that they generate better buy signals than sell signals. For the MBI, there are three buy signals that are important:

Buy Signals:

1. A penetration of MBI 45 to the upside. Obviously, the MBI will have to have fallen below 45 in order for this to occur.
2. A valid trendline break. Three peaks are necessary for a valid trendline—an initial peak and two additional peaks of descending amplitude.
3. A positive divergence between the action of the MBI and that of the market.

Figure 11 gives the values for the New York Comp, MBI, and RSI from March 28, 1988 through January 9, 1989. It is an instructive period, as all three MBI buy signals are clearly visible. Often two signals will occur together. If all three signals occur at the same time, expect a really good trade. However, don't wait for such a triple signal, as they are rare. Here are the signals.

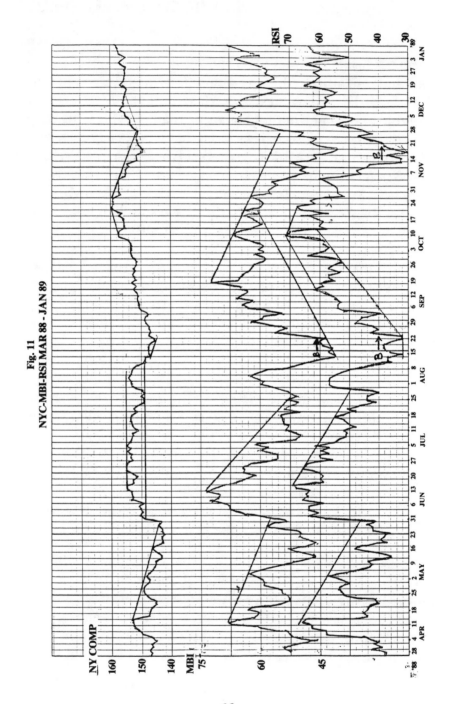

Fig. 11
NYC-MBI-RSI MAR 88 - JAN 89

1. The MBI moved from below to above 45 on August 23 and on November 21. On August 23, there was also clear-cut postive divergence with the market.
2. a. A valid trendline break occurred on May 31. Often the MBI will back off and not penetrate the down trendline as quickly after the third peak. But this early penetration does not invalidate the signal.
   b. A valid, if rather ragged, down trendline formed between September 19 and November 28. The penetration of this line led to a fine rally, which topped out (it is not shown on the chart) at 168.02 on the Comp on February 7, 1989. The New York Comp closed at 152.53 on the signal day, November 29, so this is a 10.2% rally in ten weeks. This rally will be discussed in detail in a later chapter when the RSL System is examined in action.

   This line is particularly instructive. The initial peak on which it is based occurred about half the way through the previous rally, underscoring my statement about the MBI topping out before the market. This early topping out in a good rally is a great early warning signal. Notice that the previous rally, which peaked in early June, entered a trading range rather than advancing. In addition the MBI could not develop a good secondary peak, as it did on October 10, as the momentum was not there. Be very wary of the market that starts falling right after an MBI peak (as the market did in mid-August 1981). Such declines are often severe and are characteristic of a change to a significantly bearish sentiment on the part of the market players.

Sell Signals:

   The sell signals using the MBI are not as clear-cut as the buy signals. There is, however, a characteristic formation in overbought territory that demands attention. It is the third peak formation in the MBI and it may coincide with an intermediate market top, especially if confirmed by a negative divergence from the RSI (Fig. 12). This formation is one of the two formations mentioned earlier for selling into a top. An essential ingredient of this formation is that the market has to be higher at MBI Peak 2 than it was at the original MBI Peak. This sell formation does not occur very frequently; but when it does, it offers a chance of selling at or near a market top. An almost picture perfect formation is present in Fig. 11 from 9/16/88 through 10/21/88.

Straight trendline analysis will tend to give premature sell signals. However, a trendline drawn at Gann's 45-degree angle can provide some good exit points. When I used the MBI on its own, I used trendline analysis and a zone concept, figuring the market would soon reverse once the MBI reached an overbought level. That idea worked fine in bear markets, but not nearly as well in bull markets. I now use the MBI more for entry signals and look for MBI and RSI signals to confirm each other (by both moving in the same direction) as sell signals.

STOPS

The initial MBI stop is similar to the initial RSI stop, namely a take-out of the reversal point. Once the position develops a profit, however, straight trendline analysis may be used (See Figure 11). Avoid drawing a trendline steeper than 45 degrees though, as these lines will usually provide premature signals.

SPECIALIZED SUB-INDICATORS

Terry Stewart (Joseph T. Stewart Jr.) in his book, *"Dynamic Stock Option Trading,"*[6] relied heavily on the MBI. He recommended running a 5-day moving average of the MBI, using crossing of the 5-day moving average by the MBI itself to generate signals. This specialized sub-indicator is useful in trading

FIG. 12—MBI Third Peak Formation

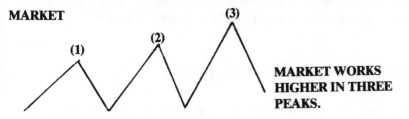

MARKET

(1) (2) (3)

**MARKET WORKS
HIGHER IN THREE
PEAKS.**

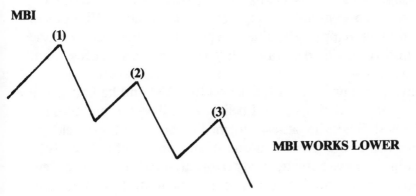

MBI

(1) (2) (3)

MBI WORKS LOWER

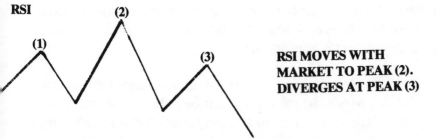

RSI

(1) (2) (3)

**RSI MOVES WITH
MARKET TO PEAK (2).
DIVERGES AT PEAK (3)**

See Fig. 11 Sept. 16 — Oct. 26 1988

markets, although using it in trending markets may result in whipsaws. But Stewart liked the MBI, calling it, "The best overall short-term indicator to measure the strength, weakness, and direction in the market at any particular time," (Page 79).

OVERALL COMMENT AND SUMMARY

Curtis Hesler, who presently owns and runs Professional Timing Service, an excellent stock market advisory (P. O. Box 7483, Missoula, MT 59807) has had some nice things to say about the MBI over the years. He's made remarks like, "This is the absolute best measure I have ever come across of the markets overbought and oversold extremes," (Issue 8902, 2/3/89). Curt took over Professional Timing Service from Larry Williams in 1984 and I am happy to be able to report that Larry also liked the MBI and referred to it favorably when he ran Professional Timing Service.

I have corresponded with Curt on the MBI and he knows the new way of calculating it, but I believe he still prefers and uses the old method. Since the patterns formed by both methods yield the same information, this is a matter of personal preference. But I am happy to have solved, to my own satisfaction, the problem caused by the advancing volume component, and I recommend the new way of calculating the MBI.

The MBI over the years has stood me in very good stead. It was the first indicator that I really came to trust and rely upon, and I am very pleased it has been accepted by market professionals. The MBI has three component indicators. A brief discussion of how each behaves is appropriate:

1. **A/D Component:** This is, of course, derived from two 10-day MA's, so values will not be liable to violent moves on a daily basis. The A/D Component has reached values as high as 26.8 (8/26/82) and as low as 2.6 (10/27/78). Most of the time, values will fall between 18 and 5.

2. **Advancing Volume Component:** This is now volume-proofed so that values have to fall between 0 and 100, with extreme readings on a daily basis of 0(10/19/87) and 95 (1/5/87), and on a 10-day MA basis, 24.9 (10/19/87) and 73.4 (1/15/87). These 10-day MA figures are divided by 3 before being entered into the MBI calculation.

3. **The TRIN Component:** On a daily basis (before October 1987), the daily TRIN usually varied between 0.45 on the bullish side and 2.8 on the bearish side. Extreme daily readings were 0.16 (8/20/82) and 4.09 (1/5/82). That was until October 19, 1987 when the daily TRIN reading was 13.86, the highest and most bearish daily reading ever by far. The previous worst reading was on Friday, October 16, when a reading of 5.78 was given. 10-day MA readings in the past would vary between 0.7 on the bullish side and 1.20 on the bearish side. The absolute highest (most bearish) 10-day MA reading before October 1987 was on 10/3/74 at 1.854. Then came October 1987, with a record 10-day MA reading of 3.949 on 10/27/87. If you haven't worked with a TRIN before, you will not be able immediately to appreciate what an unprecedented and outlandishly bearish value this was. A 10-day MA of the TRIN on the bullish side rarely falls below 0.7, doing so on 10/2/74 with a value of 0.692 and on 11/20/80 with a value of 0.615.

So the TRIN unraveled in 1987. Before 1987, using the old assigned values, which turned negative at a 10-day MA of the TRIN of 1.65, there had only been one period since 1972 that the assigned values had actually become negative. That was from 10/1/74 through 10/8/74. The ultimate bearish 10-day MA reading of 1.854 on 10/3/74 had an assigned value of −2.5. October 1987 presented me with a major problem. The 10-day MA of the TRIN hit 3.007 on October 19 and 3.949 on October 27. Logically, the MBI would have to turn negative to reflect the extreme negativity of these numbers. But the MBI was not designed ever to be negative, so it was time for an adjustment in the assigned values to be made. The new assigned values are given in Table 9. I sincerely hope we never need to use the values at the bottom end of this scale again.

One effect of this reassignment of values is that the TRIN component now contributes less to the movement of MBI than it used to. I considered dropping the TRIN component altogether, but I am glad I did not, as it balances the other two components nicely and I think it is always worth knowing what the TRIN is doing, both on the daily and the 10-day MA basis.

There is another good reason for keeping the TRIN component in the MBI. As far as I know, the MBI has not yet been programmed for intra-day futures trading on a real-time basis. But if it ever gets into one of the satellite computer programs, I believe that the short-term TRIN will contribute a valuable component to the MBI and will increase the accuracy of short-term signals.

One final point of discussion about TRIN. There is an interesting phenomenon which occurs, and I know that I am not the only technician to have noticed it. The signal is set up when the daily TRIN readings for two consecutive days total less than 1.00, providing one of the two days' readings does not reach 0.6. Table 11 gives the two-day TRIN readings that fulfill these requirements and the subsequent market action, as represented by the New York Comp one month later and three months later. The date given for the two-day TRIN combination under 1.00 is the first day, but the value of the New York Comp clearly has to be that of the second, the confirming day.

The table is most interesting. For the period 3/25/75 to 8/1/84, there are a total of eight such back-to-back bullish days. The two-day TRIN signal had real predictive value with six clear winners. It is important to remember that the great bull market started in August 1982. There were two signals in 1985, both winners, and two in 1986 that were fair enough. Then, in 1987, there were four signals that were all losers on a one-month basis and four signals in 1988— two winners, two losers. What, you may ask, is going on? I am sure you will have guessed the answer. Namely, program trading.

Table 11
TRIN: 2 DAY < 1.00

	DAY 1	DAY 2	NYC DAY 2	1/12 LATER	3/12 LATER	+ −
3.25.75	0.52	0.42	44.31	45.95	50.51	+2
12.22.77	0.47	0.51	52.26	49.38	47.86	−2
5.11.78	0.43	0.54	54.85	55.89	58.53	+2
5.16.79	0.58	0.41	56.23	57.26	61.70	+2
11.9.79	0.47	0.41	58.82	61.58	67.51	+2
11.11.80	0.48	0.43	77.44	74.16	73.05	−2
8.20.82	0.16	0.47	66.36	70.98	77.12	+2
8.1.84	0.42	0.47	90.77	94.76	96.48	+2
5.9.85	0.49	0.48	106.64	109.83	109.66	+2
10.11.85	0.49	0.44	107.64	113.82	118.82	+2
8.11.86	0.37	0.43	140.02	132.81	141.89	0
11.20.86	0.31	0.37	140.94	142.65	162.82	+2
5.4.87	0.54	0.40	166.34	166.16	177.39	0
8.10.87	0.30	0.45	186.13	177.46	134.06	−2
10.20.87	0.25	0.39	143.02	135.56	136.72	−2
11.11.87	0.58	0.35	138.68	134.79	143.99	0
4.22.88	0.32	0.43	148.21	142.21	149.25	0
5.31.88	0.22	0.48	150.34	153.68	148.29	0
6.21.88	0.44	0.47	155.34	150.90	153.61	−2
8.16.88	0.40	0.46	147.64	152.79	149.35	+2
3.2.89	0.41	.0.56	163.90	166.43	181.49	+2

Like death and taxes, as a trader one has to learn to live with this market phenomenon. Program trading can cause some very sharp market moves in either direction. These violent moves are the bane of a switch-fund trader's life. Their appearance in the marketplace forced me to examine ways of avoiding, as far as possible, the damage they cause. What materialized was the RSL System as a formal approach to trading the market.

Many technicians I know prefer switching 100% into the market on buy signals and 100% out on sells. That approach is fine when the market doesn't move more than, say, 1.5% - 2% on a daily basis. But program trading can result in horrendously large moves, like the 6.9% drop on January 8, 1988, already alluded to. There is no other explanation to account for these violent intra-day swings, particularly if the market does not follow through, giving rise to what I call an "aberrant day."

Just what is an "aberrant day?" It is a violent move against a prevailing trend that exists as a one-day phenomenon. It is clearly related to program trading. For one day to qualify as an aberrant day, the market, on the next day, has to resume the trend as though nothing had happened. The day cannot be recognized, therefore, until the close of the next market day. I should stress that we are basically talking about violent down days in an uptrend, as such days have great impact on mutual fund switch traders. The problem, of course, is that the aberrant day often triggers sell signals; and if the signal is on a 100% in/100% out-type system, the trader may get badly whipsawed.

Using the RSL System, an aberrant day will often trigger some sell signals, especially in the most sensitive indicators. But the fact that the indicators trigger at different levels offers a significant measure of protection so that most of the position will be retained. The aberrant day shows up with stunning clarity on charts of index futures. The market on an aberrant day characteristically gaps lower on the open and then proceeds to take out an uptrend line. Such action *should* trigger a reversal and will certainly trigger some sell signals. The problem is that once the programs have gone through with thunder and lightning, the sunshine comes out and the market resumes its original trend. Figure 13 shows a typical aberrant day. I am sure more aberrant days will occur in the future.

This is why I no longer believe, if I ever did, on moving in and out on a 100% basis in a switch-fund program. And as an aside, it is this program-generated volatility that knocks the you-know-what out of the mechanical short-term futures trading systems for the S&P and the NYFE. Such short-term systems must use reasonably close stops and there is just no way of building the aberrant day into a short-term mechanical system without allowing far too much action against the position. By this time you will gather that I am mightily displeased with program trading which serves no useful purpose for the general investing public. It is merely an arbitrage device for those with big bucks to profit from market disparities on a more or less riskless basis. But I am pleased that the MBI has now been revised to cope with the markedly increased total trading volume, and we will next examine how the MBI backs up the RSI in locating good trades.

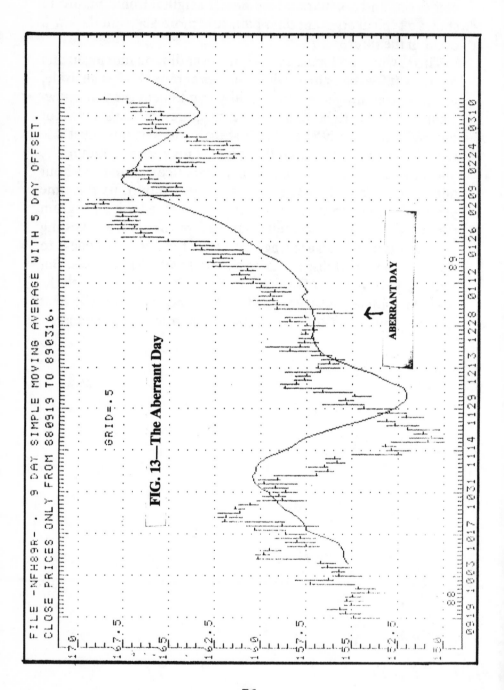

FIG. 13—The Aberrant Day

Chapter 3

The Role Of The RSI
And The MBI
In The RSL System

The RSI will provide a figure for each day's market action. The extreme readings to date are 11 and 84, although values of 30 on the low side and 70 on the high side will contain most of the action of the market, representing normally oversold and overbought areas, respectively. Each market day, after the close of trading, it will be possible to obtain an RSI reading. The actual values will be most helpful in assessing the validity of any other signals received from the other RSL System indicators. I decided to use the RSI as the "locator" or point indicator rather than the MBI (since the MBI had to be reworked after the crash of October 1987). This meant that I did not have a solid body of back data for the new way of calculating the MBI (without having to do a great deal of work). Since I already had excellent data for the RSI going back to 1980, the RSI was the logical choice.

However, that is not to say that the MBI does not provide useful backup data, because it certainly does so. The RSI has to rise if the market rises and vice versa. Not so the MBI, as this indicator reflects the crucial differences between the latest day's market action and that of the market ten trading days previously. The MBI can increase in value on a day when the market itself declines and vice versa. This can provide a useful early warning sign that a trend change may be in the offing.

There are two indicators in the RSL System that give unequivocal buy and sell signals as they are purely mathematical with no interpretation of any sort involved. These two indicators are:

1. A simple 21-day moving average offset by 5 days, the 21/5 indicator.

2. A 0.1 exponential MA of the advance/decline line, the 0.1 A/D Indicator.

These indicators will be discussed in full later, but I mention them here as part of the five vital values on which the RSL System master worksheet is based. The five daily core values for the master worksheet are:

1. Value of the New York Comp (closing basis).
2. RSI value.
3. MBI value.
4. 21/5 buy-sell signals.
5. 0.1 A/D buy-sell signals.

The master worksheet, Table 12, is presented now so that the other indicators can be discussed (from those that trigger in highly oversold RSI territory to those triggering much closer to midrange). The idea, remember, is to phase into the market as the RSI moves up from oversold to overbought. The RSL System master worksheet will leave no doubt about what the market is doing. All that is required is a daily update of all the indicators (see Table 17 for actual market data).

You will notice that all buy signals are entered into the left-hand columns. The core data is entered into the central columns. And all sell signals are to the right of this data. The final column

Table 12
RSL SYSTEM
Master Work Sheet

New Buy Signals	Total Buy	NYC	RSI	MBI	21/5	0.1A/D	New Sell Signals	Total Sell	Net B-S

gives the net of all buy signals *minus* all sell signals. I would stress that the total number of signals, that is, buy signals plus sell signals, is not finite. There will be occasions when the specialized sub-indicators kick in (for instance, RSI - SI. When this indicator kicks in at RSI 74, it stays active. It stays on buy until the market falls to RSI 50. Such a fall is not a sell signal for the whole market, just an exit signal for the RSI - SI. The total number of indicators on buy will fall by one, but the number of sell indicators will not increase once the RSI - SI is no longer in effect. Note also that the parent indicator can only give a signal once even though, as we have seen, there are three buy signals for the MBI. But when one of them is given, an additional MBI signal does not count as an additional buy signal. So, for example, the MBI signal on November 29 in Table 17 is in parentheses because a valid MBI buy was already in effect from November 22.

There will also be occasions when the RSI and/or MBI should be counted as neutral rather than on buy or sell. This is to a certain extent a judgment call. As an example, let us assume the last clearcut signal was a sell and the RSI and the MBI have both fallen into the low midrange, approaching oversold. At this point, the market starts to rally without generating clearcut buy signals on either indicator. On such occasions, each indicator should be counted as neutral when the readings reach midrange rather than still being counted on a sell. Of the other RSL indicators, only the $W(D)^{10}$ should be judged neutral. This would occur when, after giving a sell, it fails to generate a subsequent buy formation before moving up over 0. When this happens, it should be ranked neutral. So we have three indicators capable of being judged neutral:

1. RSI.
2. MBI.
3. $W(D)^{10}$ (See Chapter 4).

And five that are always on buy or sell:

1. 21/5.
2. 0.1 A/D.
3. Single-width envelope indicator (SW). ⎫
4. Double-width envelope indicator (DW). ⎬ (See Chapter 5)
5. NAT indicators (see Chapters 6 and 8). ⎭

This is fortunate. Even when the first group of indicators is listed as neutral, there still have to be more indicators on one side of the market than the other once you've analyzed the second group. This is useful for assessing the trend. But remember—using the RSL System, the first unit is put down on a valid signal from one of the indicators (usually the $W(D)^{10}$) so that the net buy-sell score will be still negative at -6.

The RSI and MBI have already been discussed. The other indicators in the RSL System kick in from oversold readings of the RSI at the bottom of the scale to values that move the RSI into midrange or even overbought territory. They are:

	6. Envelope Indicator double-width (DW).
RSI midrange	5. 21/5 MA indicator.
	4. 0.1 A/D indicator.
RSI rising ↑	3. NAT indicator.
	2. Envelope indicator single-width (SW).
RSI oversold	1. $W(D)^{10}$ indicator.

We have seen that the RSI-SI kicks in as a buy in quite overbought RSI territory. I would emphasize that the main indicators give signals as the RSI moves from oversold to midrange. The $W(D)^{10}$ signal can only occur, if it occurs, in oversold territory and will usually trigger before the other indicators. The formation may never occur. If it does, the first unit should be placed on the table as soon as the formation is complete. I have found the signal, if it forms, to be very reliable. Following the signal gives the mutual fund trader an edge on the market, as the $W(D)^{10}$ signal characteristically triggers in "quiet" market periods. It will also usually do so before that violent upday that so often triggers the other indicators, but which offers no profit to the mutual fund trader following the slower indicators (as a trader not in the market on such a day can only enter at the end of the day).

When the first indicator gives a valid signal confirmed by its position on the RSI, the first unit should be traded. It is easy to talk oneself out of taking action on the grounds that there may be a better place to enter later. Don't listen to the demon suggesting this; put the money down. And if you feel uncomfortable about doing so because of your assessment of what the market "should" do, that is probably so much the better.

Where money is involved, I am a cautious person by nature and I am very cautious in trading other people's money. It is only on rare occasions that I get all four units working for my discretionary accounts. This is partly because of the size of the accounts, but also their stated purpose. Namely, to assure a happy retirement; and in such an account, preservation of capital is of vital importance. But, for anyone with some discretionary money, I advise getting all four units working in a way I will discuss a little in this chapter and more fully in Chapter 9, *The RSL System in Action.* The indicators will not always trigger in the sequence given earlier in this chapter, of course. But the RSI and MBI have to move up in value for them to be able to do so; and the failure of these indicators to advance nicely should be taken as a warning that the rally could abort. Ideally, using the RSL System, this scenario goes as follows:

1. RSI and MBI significantly oversold, RSI around 30, MBI below 45.
2. W(D)^{10} signal, first unit bought.
3. RSI or MBI buy, second unit bought. We now have two units in action and five other main indicators to choose from. Obviously, the quicker the other two units get into action, the better will be the final profit, providing the rally continues. If the rally continues, valid buy signals will be

received from all the other indicators. Choosing between them all becomes a matter of personal choice. The reason that there are more indicators (8) than units (4) is to give the trader the best chance of getting reliable signals as early as possible in a rally.

It's easier to get all four units working if the market starts in oversold territory, so that buy signals from the W(D)^{10} and either the RSI or the MBI are possible. But some good rallies start from a trading range breakout from midrange. In these instances it can be difficult to climb on board fully. Just remember, the market can rally any time and from anywhere it wants. But I believe firmly in waiting for valid signals from the RSL indicators before taking any action. You'll find some excellent profits and trading opportunities by following the signals. You don't need to "jump ahead" to make good money.

It is very frustrating to go "flat the market" before going on vacation, only to return to find the market has rallied substantially, putting all the RSL indicators on a buy while you're not trading. (It has happened to me on several occasions). All you can do is wait either for an RSI-SI signal (but don't go with more than one unit) or for the next correction. If I cannot take action the day of (or the day following) a valid signal, I do not believe in chasing that signal. I like to have a valid W(D)^{10} buy signal and a buy from either the RSI or MBI before going with the remaining two units. The next indicator to trigger, if it has not already gone on buy, is usually the envelope indicator, single-width (SW).

4. Envelope indicator, single-width (SW) goes on buy; a third unit is bought.
5. The last unit is put down when the next indicator goes on buy, say the 0.1 A/D.
6. The 0.1 A/D goes on buy and the fourth and final unit is now bought. The full position has been achieved. But the full four units can only be reached if the market rallies sufficiently to trigger the RSL indicators.

When should the position be unwound? The answer is simple. The units are sold when their individual stops are hit. This will often mean the last unit bought will be the first one sold. Each unit will have a different exit point and that exit point will trigger trading action. Of course, if the market gets badly hit, it may happen that the stops for more than one unit are activated. But I again stress the importance of thinking of each unit as a unit —with its own exit points based on that individual indicator.

If you trade in a family of funds, it is possible to assign each unit to a different fund and to move that unit on an all-or-none basis. Fund management will try to discourage what it considers to be excessive switching, so it may be more difficult to trade mutual funds in the future using the RSL System. But where there is a will, there is a way; and if necessary, a number of different fund groups could be utilized. This will not be possible in retirement plans to any extent unless the trader has more than one plan. But for post-tax trading of funds, the concept of using not only a number of funds within a single fund family, but also a number of different fund families makes a great deal of sense.

Doing so will grant the mutual fund trader the freedom to move if and when the indicators say so without worrying about any other consideration. It is mentally difficult to sell a unit soon after it has been purchased, but it has to be done even occasionally the very next day after purchase if the appropriate indicator triggers. I have only had to do that once in my years of trading, but sell I did, feeling foolish to be sure, but happy to be following my system. The more one can feel a prisoner of one's system and indicators, the better the results will be. It is worth repeating that the purpose of keeping indicators is to utilize them, not second-guess them.

This then gives an outline of how important the RSI and MBI are in locating when the other indicators may be expected to trigger. We will now examine the remaining indicators.

Chapter 4

The W(D)^{10} Indicator

PRINCIPLE

This indicator is based on a 0.15 exponential MA of the NY Comp. Calculating an exponential MA is easy (see calculation). The indicator plots the difference between the NY Comp itself and its 0.15 exponential MA. The indicator will be positive when the market, *which is always considered first,* has a value greater than its 0.15 exponential MA, and negative when the NY Comp has a value below that of its 0.15 exponential MA.

This indicator works because markets, when they get oversold, do not actually reverse on a dime (though at times appearing to do so). There is usually a subtle backing and filling period which shows up very nicely on the W(D)^{10} Indicator. This is the only action of the market on the buy side that the indicator seeks to identify.

TECHNIQUE

Necessary Data:

The closing values of the NY Comp are recorded and a 0.15 exponential MA is calculated. The 0.15 exponential MA will need about 15 market days to stabilize. The W(D)^{10} Indicator plots the difference between the market and its 0.15 exponential MA.

Calculation:

Assume that the original 0.15 exponential moving value is identical to the closing value of the NY Comp on the first day of calculation. Again we will use the January 1989 data. On January 3, the NY Comp closed at 154.98. The 0.15 exponential moving average is assigned this value. On January 4, the NY Comp closed at 157.06. The new 0.15 exponential MA figure is derived as follows: (157.06 − 154.98) 0.15 + 154.98 = 155.29. That is, 0.15 of the difference between the NY Comp closing value on January 4 and the exponential MA value on January 3 is applied to the exponential MA value on January 3 to give the new value on January 4. Notice in order to start the calculation we arbitrarily assign the closing value on January 3 as its exponential MA value. On January 5, the NY Comp closed at 157.49. The calculation is as follows: (157.49 − 155.29) 0.15 + 155.29 = 155.62. The value of 155.29 represents the 0.15 exponential MA value for January 4, with the new value for January 5 being 155.62.

Since this is an exponential moving average, the average has to advance (become more positive or less negative) as the market advances and decline (become less positive or more negative) as the market declines. Table 13 gives the 0.15 exponential moving average for the first 14 trading days of January and the W(D)^{10} Indicator value obtained by subtracting the 0.15 exponential MA value from the value of the NY Comp itself. At the end of 14 trading days, the value of the 0.15 exponential value was 159.30. The true 0.15 exponential MA based on a much longer data base was 159.38 so, for practical purposes, the indicator has stabilized.

ACTION SIGNALS

The indicator represents the difference between the NY Comp

and its 0.15 exponential MA. The critical buy formation occurs as follows:

1. The indicator falls to − $2.00. that is, the NY Comp has a value $2.00 less than the value of its 0.15 exponential MA. This value will be referred to as − 2.00.

2. The indicator rises above − 2.00.

3. There is a fall again to − 2.00 or very close to it. The first down limb has to be below − 2.00. The second limb of the W formation has to be close, but it is not absolutely essential for this limb to fall below − 2.00. It is, however, essenttial that there be a retreat to set up the full W formation (Figure 14).

4. The buy is a take out of the intermediate area (Figure 15). This is the only buy signal the indicator generates. An initial − 2.00 or greater reading is necessary for it to occur. This will mean the market will be oversold and the RSI will confirm this. I do not have on record a valid W(D)^{10} buy signal occurring when the RSI was not oversold. It is clear that the RSI does provide important confirmation and the RSI value is part of the decision-making process.

Note that a valid W(D)^{10} buy signal can be set up even if the indicator falls into deeply oversold territory, provided there is a $1.50 upmove from the low point, then a good retracement followed by a takeout of the intermediate limb.

On the sell side, there are two signals:

1. A divergence between the action of the market and the W(D)^{10} Indicator with the following characteristics:
   A. An indicator peak above + 3.00.
   B. A 9-day minimum trading day interval followed by:
   C. A second peak above + 3.00 with negative divergence from the market.

Table 13
0.15 EXPONENTIAL MA + W(D)^{10} INDICATOR

		NY COMP CLOSE	0.15 EXP MA	W(D)^{10} VALUE
1	Jan 3	154.98	154.98	0
2	4	157.06	155.29	+ 1.77
3	5	157.49	155.62	+ 1.87
4	6	157.96	155.97	+ 1.99
5	9	158.15	156.30	+ 1.85
6	10	157.85	156.53	+ 1.32
7	11	158.65	156.85	+ 1.80
8	12	159.26	157.21	+ 2.05
9	13	159.58	157.57	+ 2.01
10	16	159.78	157.90	+ 1.88
11	17	159.48	158.14	+ 1.34
12	18	161.01	158.57	+ 2.44
13	19	161.26	158.97	+ 2.29
14	20	161.16	159.30	+ 1.86

FIG. 14
W(D)^{10} Indicator
Initial Formation

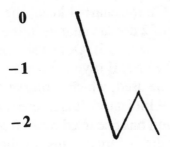

FIG. 15
W(D)^{10} Indicator
Buy Formation

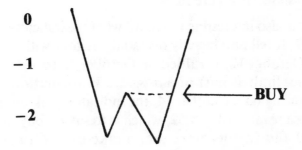

This formation does not happen very frequently. It is for this reason that the D is in parenthesis. D, of course, stands for divergence. But when it does occur, it offers a quite excellent exit point. The formation can be clearly seen in Figure 16.

2. A penetration of the *10° trendline* drawn off the second limb of the W. This 10° line is, of course, quite arbitrary. But importantly, it works. On the charts I keep, the 10° trendline advances at the rate of 2 dollars change in the indicator for each 21 trading days (Figure 16). Obviously, the scale determines the pitch of the line. But you can see that a 10° line works well on the scale used, which is one small square per dollar for the W(D)^{10} Indicator. It is interesting to note the W(D)^{10} buy formation has occurred more frequently since October 1987 than it did before it. This, I believe, relates to the general bullishness of the earlier period and the fact that values of -2.00 and below occurred less frequently. Of course, the warning must be given that it may never work again, but seriously I doubt that. I have details of the indicator going back to 1981 and I have on record only one instance of an immediate failure of the indicator. This was on February 14, 1984 when the market backed off for three days before mounting a six-day rally. But, I admit the best signals have been post-October 1987, with two marvelous signals shown in Figure 16.

It is also interesting to record what the indicator did in October 1987. It fell into heavily oversold territory with a value of -4.54 on October 12. It rallied on October 13 to -1.73 to set up the initial limb as part of a *possible* W formation. However, the following day, October 14, the indicator took out its reversal low with a reading of -5.52, which is to say *no* buy signal was generated and furthermore that a take-out of a reversal point in oversold territory was (and is) a strong sell (Figure 17). For my two managed accounts, as I detailed earlier, I was safely out of the market at that time and in cash. The point I am trying to make is that those who bought the market in that period were doing so on a wish and a prayer. Both were misdirected.

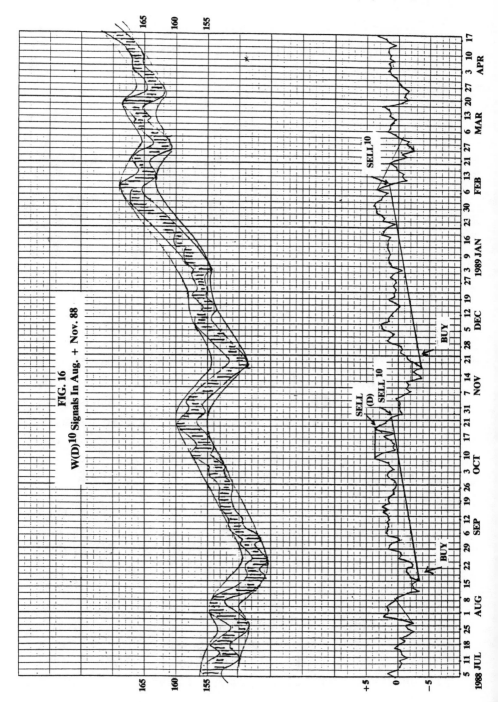

FIG. 16
W(D)^{10} Signals In Aug. + Nov. 88

Fig. 17
W(D)^{10} FORMATION IN OCTOBER 1987

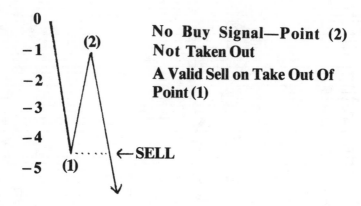

No Buy Signal—Point (2)
Not Taken Out

A Valid Sell on Take Out Of
Point (1)

Followers of the RSL System would have been in cash or short, as there were no valid buys on any of the indicators. When it comes right down to it, playing the market consists, to a large extent, of not trying to outsmart the market. Frankly, I "hate" to put money down on the table on a strongly up day. The "hate" is a throwback to the old haphazard days. I have learned to take buy signals in overbought territory, but I'll admit it wasn't easy. Indeed, *this is not an easy game.* It is terrifically tempting—when a big buy program has gone through and popped the market up 70 points or so—to say to oneself, particularly if it is a Friday, "I'll wait to see what happens on Monday." The problem is that Monday may be down and the inactivity seems justified as Tuesday is flat. (Beware the little voice inside oneself that says, "You've got the touch.") But then Wednesday takes off with another 50+ point blast. And sure as shooting, if it was difficult deciding to go on Friday, it is going to be that much more difficult to get aboard on Wednesday. I have learned over the years to go when the indicators say, "Go." *Pay no attention whatsoever* to the GNP or unemployment figures, the predictions about interest rates, or the money supply numbers. The market may well respond to them in contrary fashion anyway. And besides, the guesses the "pundits" make are at times so far off the mark as to make any market decision based on what they predict hazardous to one's financial health. The more you can program yourself to act as a computer would act, the better your results will be. Nobody has any difficulty in "paper-trading." Paper-trading is like miniature golf; it has no relationship to the real thing. *You have to put the money down* and it has to be done on some conviction or other. I believe that indicators such as the W(D)^{10} form the best basis for convictions. When all is said and done, it is the bottom line that counts. The indicators I use and have used over the years make money. They may or may not be the absolute best indicators, but it is for certain sure they work. I have grown very comfortable with them and know they work.

The value of this book will be to give you a shortcut to confidence in the indicators described here. There is some fun to be had, no doubt about it, in "fiddling around" with someone else's indicators to see if they can be improved upon. The danger is taking credit for the improvements when the improvements are successful, while blaming the basic indicators when they are not. I believe all traders should experiment with their own ideas. What I am presenting here is a system and a bunch of indicators that have stood the test of real-time trading.

It would seem to be very elementary to state that you cannot win if you haven't got a bet down. The difficulty is getting the bet down. And I stress that it is a bet; and because the eventual outcome is never known, it is gambling. The differences between casino gambling and gambling in the stock market are subtle but real. If I go to a craps table, it will be a single craps table in a casino with many. At this table, the dice may be running hot or cold. It is important that I try to identify the trend of the dice, just as it is that I try to identify the trend of the market. The major difference is that the dice on my table may be "hot" and on the table next to it, be "cold." This does not happen in the market, when all the action is basically on one big table.

There is also another very important consideration. Most, but not all, bets in the casino are contract bets. Simply stated, this means that a bet once down rides to a decision and cannot be removed. The bet either wins or loses. Fortunately, in the stock and futures markets, it is possible to pull the bet off the table so that the entire bet is not lost. It is this feature that makes gambling in the market actually safer than gambling in the casino, providing that strict rules for money management are followed. It takes no skill at all to be a compulsive gambler or drinker. The skill involved is taking the fun and avoiding the pain. The French have a wonderful phrase, "Toute chose appartient à qui sait en jouir (Andre Gide)," which says, "Everything belongs to the person who knows how to enjoy it."

The market has been very carefully designed to avoid the appearance of gambling. My view is that there is nothing wrong with gambling. When I thought of myself as an investor, my results were horrible. And they only began to improve when I thought of myself as a gambler, whoops, I mean trader, and developed some trading indicators. And, of course, there is absolutely no point in keeping indicators unless you are prepared to follow them wherever they may lead. The rules have to be formulated and followed. If the indicator goes through a bad period, a careful analysis is in order. No indicator works all the time. An attempt should be made to identify why it is not working. This may or may not be possible. But fortunately, with the RSL System we have a number of indicators at our disposal. We only build up to a full position in the market if the market by its own action triggers buy signals at increasingly higher RSI levels.

STOPS

The initial stop is a take out of the second limb of the W formation.

The stop is based on the W(D)^{10} indicator, not on the action of the market. This stop has never been activated as an immediate event in any of my historical analysis, including the period mentioned in 1984. This is with nothing optimized. The subsequent stop is a break in the 10° trendline (or a valid (D) signal).

SPECIALIZED SUB-INDICATORS

None.

OVERALL COMMENT AND SUMMARY

I am very pleased with this indicator, as it triggers in a "quiet" market period and enables the mutual fund trader to take a position at a time when the market is not "frothy." This indicator picks up the first sign of strength in an oversold market and will usually trigger before the other RSL indicators. Of course, it cannot trigger unless the W formation occurs, with the market falling to -2.00 below its 0.15 exponential MA. So there will be rallies that start without it. This is not a major problem as there are other indicators in our quiver.

The W(D)^{10} formation provides a basic buy formation. For the exit points, either the D configuration or a penetration of the 10° trendline will also offer some useful sell short signals for those traders playing the short side of the market. There are four simple ways of betting on a market decline:

1. Sell a futures contract short, hoping to buy it back later for a profit.
2. Buy put options. You will pay a time premium, but all that is at stake is the option premium paid.
3. Sell call options. The maximum profit will be realized if the call expires worthless. The risk, however, is unlimited.

4. Short individual stocks. This is not as highly recommended, as stocks have to be sold on an uptick or zero uptick and the short seller is debited any dividends.

There are a group of mutual funds called closed-end funds (because they have a finite number of shares when issued). No additional shares can be issued, such as occurs in the more common open-end mutual funds. These closed-end funds are traded like common stocks, usually on the Big Board. And like common stocks, they may be shorted. Why not short them when the RSL signals go on sell, thereby hoping to profit from the market's downside action? There are two very good reasons not to:

1. These funds often sell at a discount to net asset value (NAV) and it is folly to short an undervalued asset. Undervaluation will help maintain the price during a down move.
2. The short seller is debited any dividends paid. The ideal short candidate is an overvalued stock paying no dividend.

The W(D)^{10} indicator, then, is a great indicator on its own. It gives rise to some great position trades, as can be seen in Figure 16. Such trades will be examined later in Chapter 9, but I would recommend this signal to all market players, be they mutual fund traders or those trading options or futures. The only problems with it are:

1. Not every rally by any means starts with a valid signal.
2. The signals are at best several weeks or even months apart.

Chapter 5

The Envelope Indicators

PRINCIPLE

There are two indicators using the envelope system, a single width indicator (SW) and a double width indicator (DW). The former always triggers before the latter. Indeed, often significantly before the latter. The two indicators will be considered together, as they are based on the envelope concept described by J.M. Hurst in his book *"The Profit Magic of Stock Transaction Timing."* [7] This is without question one of the most important books ever written on the market. Before program trading entered the market scene with its attendant unwelcome volatility, I know I could have (and in fact at times did) make money using the envelope indicators alone.

What do the envelopes do? Perhaps I should state first what they are and what they are not. First, envelopes are not figured on a certain percentage above and below a moving average. These are trading bands (though they may be called envelopes). There is a well known system that takes a 21 day moving average of the Dow and draws trading bands at plus or minus 4% above and below this average. There are rules for trading band penetration

97

and mid-range retracement. There is no doubt that the system, which has 8 buy signals and 8 sell signals can and does work (it is called the Peerless System and was developed by W.C. Schmidt). This system is based on a non-centered moving average. Moving averages will always lag the values they follow, unless they are displaced backwards one half span (i.e. centered). This is because the average relates to all the values. It is clear that using an 11 day moving average, the average value relates to day 6 with 5 days

1 2 3 4 5 <u>6</u> 7 8 9 10 11

days data before and 5 days data after day 6. Hurst discussed this centered moving average idea at length in his book, but what evolved for me was the concept of envelopes that could be drawn to include the known values. These envelopes are remarkably similar to trading bands calculated around a *centered* moving average. But the envelopes can be drawn without having to calculate the moving average itself. Envelopes drawn by the rules that I will give in a moment are remarkable analytical tools. They are flexible and in bending but not easily breaking they will conform to the dominant underlying moving average without the trader having to identify this moving average. It is this changing flexible nature that presents a major problem in the computerization of the envelope indicators.

The single width envelope signals will respond to the short term swings in the market and in a trading market will tend to whipsaw. The double width envelope signals will do a great job of picking up the primary trend of the market and will provide valid RSL system signals on their own. Such signals will be at higher RSI levels than the single width signals. Both SW and DW signals give entry points for The RSL system. As we have noted, there are several indicators to choose from. The trick is to use them all and go with the earliest valid signal since *all* the indicators in the system are reliable. Sometimes the 0.1 A/D will trigger before the DW envelope signal, sometimes after it. Also, sometimes the 21/5 will kick in before either. The RSL system is a "go with the flow" system and is capable of extracting considerable profit

98

from the market at reduced risk. Envelopes work because markets trend (although of course not all the time). Each day the market will establish a high and a low and the distance between these two points will fluctuate about a mean. Envelopes can be drawn on any time frame. We are using a daily bar chart when applying the RSL System. If the market behavior changes from a period of lower highs and lower lows to a phase of higher highs and higher lows, the envelopes will reflect this change. Although the true range of the market will vary on a daily basis, *there is no way that the market can advance without turning the SW envelope to the upside.* And it is the penetration of the projected upper part of the envelope that triggers the buy. The penetration of the lower part of the envelope triggers the sell. A study of Figure 16, where both the SW and DW envelopes are drawn, shows the broad sweep of the DW indicator and the much more choppy nature of the SW indicator. Figure 18 shows a close-up of the signals which are similar to trendline breaks but actually are envelopes. Envelopes are *not* trendlines and are much more flexible.

FIG. 18
SW and DW Envelope Signals

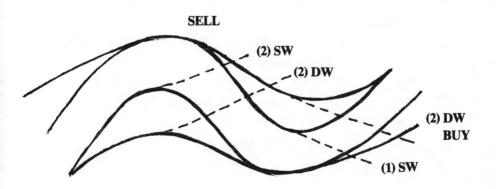

SELL

(2) SW

(2) DW

(2) DW
BUY

(1) SW

TECHNIQUE

Necessary Data

The high, low, and close values are plotted daily using bar charts. Envelopes are drawn to include market activity. Figure 16 shows how the envelopes follow in the market. Figure 16 is a copy of one of my daily charts and shows exactly how I draw both SW and DW indicators.

Calculation

None. No math is involved. Signals are generated directly from the charts. The rules of envelope analysis are:

1. Envelope boundaries are always parallel to each other (or as close to parallel as possible).

2. Envelopes fold over gradually. Be careful particularly on a down turn that you do not draw a trendline. Envelopes are defined by tops in an uptrend and bottoms in a downtrend (unlike trendlines).

3. The present trend is in effect until a valid envelope signal in the reverse direction is received.

4. The close must always be within the envelope. Highs and lows may be cut off. This usually will occur only as the envelope changes direction.

5. The double width envelope seldom runs for any distance with the single width envelope.

6. The double width envelope may be somewhat more than double the single width envelope, but should not be much less than that amount.

7. "Nesting" envelopes provide very valid signals on a breakout from the nest. (See Specialized Sub-Indicator Env-SI).

8. The best signals are from sharp penetrations of the envelope. Rounding bottom (top) signals are not as clearcut.
9. When the envelope changes direction, start with an angle equivalent to but opposite from that of the previous envelope. But if a rounding bottom (top) develops give the envelope enough room to fold over gently.
10. Envelopes may be redrawn once to include the latest market action. But do not redraw them again.

Comment

The trick to drawing good looking envelopes is to learn to relax the hand.

ACTION SIGNALS

The signals are very simple. Use the NY Comp. as the base index and draw the envelopes. A *close* above the next day's projected envelope top plus $.25 is a buy using the single width envelope. A close below the next day's projected bottom minus $.25 is a sell. There is a certain amount of subjectivity in the actual drawing of the envelopes and the $.25 cushion may be increased by the individual trader if desired. The double width signal is given in the same way. Figure 18 shows how the signals are generated. In the RSL System the SW signal will be received before the DW signal, and is often the first signal to go after the W(D)[10]. I use the SW signal in my own trading very frequently. I always like to have a unit riding with this signal, often adding an additional unit when the DW envelope signal is received. This depends on the total stake and when the other RSL indicators have kicked in.

STOPS

In mutual fund switching, the stops are the sell signals. If you

101

are using envelope signals to trade futures, valid short signals are given when the envelope turns over and switches to a sell. There is an important concept to have in mind when using both single and double width envelopes. If the double width envelope has gone solidly into an uptrend, it is usually advantageous to use the stop *on the DW envelope* rather than the SW envelope now that the markets are more volatile. You will see in Chapter 9 how using the DW stop paid out in trading the November '88 rally.

SPECIALIZED SUB-INDICATORS

There are two specialized sub-indicators based on the SW envelope.

1. The Nesting Envelope (ENV. S-1).

Quite frequently, within a well defined trend the market will enter a quiet period which I call a nest. A nesting envelope will be formed over a market period of not less than, but usually not much more than, 4 trading days. In an uptrend a valid nest will form when the *highs* of the 4 days are very close to each other in value. The breakout from this nest to the upside is a very good continuation buy signal. Why don't we examine a nest that formed in January '89? The nest occurred with the highs as follows:

	High
January 5, 1989	158.16
January 6, 1989	158.59
January 9, 1989	158.56
January 10, 1989	158.45
January 11, 1989	158.65

On January 12, 1989 the market had the following high, low, and close numbers:

High	159.93	
Low	158.64	
Close	159.26	(Figure 16)

This is a *perfect* envelope nesting signal. It has the following characteristics: 1) the low of the signal was close to the previous day's high and 2) the high of the day and 3) all the day's action was for practical purposes clearly above the nest. The nest, by the way, is an *envelope* not a trading range, so the upper rim of the envelope that defines the nest will be downtrended by day 4. This was a glorious signal, so of course I went with it. The RSI at that time was very close to overbought (RSI 68). The MBI at 76 was already overbought. Indeed, the RSI went on to generate an RSI-SI buy on January 26. But I went with the signal on January 12 (before the close of trading on January 12, 1989) as it was clear the market had broken out of its nest on the upside. And I have, of course, the confirmation slip to back up my claim.

The same formation occurs in the downtrend, though not as frequently. In a downtrend, the lows of 4 trading days have to group together with little variation on their value. In 1984, from Jan. 30 through Feb. 2, such a nest formed in a clearly downtrended market. On Feb. 3, 1984, there was a clear penetration of the nest to the downside. The market on the day of the signal was down 7% from its recent high, but the nesting envelope signal led to a further decline of 5.2%.

These signals represent if not sure thing trading signals, then something awfully close to it. Anyone trading futures should wait for high probability signals. The nesting envelope signal is one with a high probability of success. Notice, by the way, in Figure 16 there were two other nesting buy signals, one on January 18, 1989, which was successful and the second on February 2, which is not. However, this latter signal would definitely be suspect for two reasons:

1. Because it occurred late in a good market move. The most reliable nesting envelope signals occur relatively early in a market move.

103

2. Two previous nesting envelope signals, both successful, had been given. A third signal is unusual and has a low success rate.

2. The Parabolic Envelope (ENV-SII)

This formation is not common, but when it does occur it will provide a second way of selling into strength (the MBI providing the other). As the market advances it may begin to lose momentum. If this occurs, a Parabolic Envelope may be formed (Figure 19). At point A the low of the day will be, indeed *must* be, on the lower boundary of the envelope. At point B the distance from the vertical will have increased to at least 1.75 times the distance between point A and the vertical. Point A and B are identified *at point B,* point A being that place where the momentum begins to slacken. The number of trading days between these two points is found, in this case 3 trading days. The projected top is therefore likely to occur on the third trading day after point B. The same formation may be seen on weekly and even on monthly charts. Indeed, it is probably easier to spot on these charts than on daily charts.

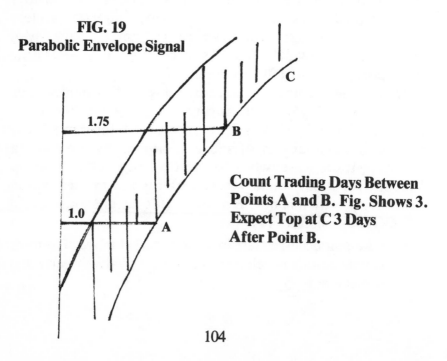

FIG. 19
Parabolic Envelope Signal

1.75

B

C

1.0

A

Count Trading Days Between Points A and B. Fig. Shows 3. Expect Top at C 3 Days After Point B.

This signal is most useful as an exit point in an up mark Although the same formation in reverse may be seen at market bottoms, such a formation should not be used for market entry as the market can still be considered to be downtrended at that point. Such an entry would qualify as bottom fishing, which is never part of the RSL System.

OVERALL COMMENT AND SUMMARY

I began to feel I definitely had a handle on the market when I became adept at drawing envelopes. The skill is not difficult to acquire, but some mental flexibility is necessary. Some traders prefer trendlines because they are always straight and unambiguous. It is worth pointing out, though, that envelope signals—particularly those from the SW envelope—will usually provide better and earlier entry signals than those from trendline analysis.

I allow myself to redraw an envelope once if it becomes clear that the original envelope could not include some new market data. But I never redraw a second time and I never redraw by very much. I prefer to let the envelope change direction under those circumstances, even if a possible whipsaw is set up by doing so.

Envelopes seek to encompass most, but not necessarily all, the activity of any given market segment within their boundaries. The boundaries are really "best-fit" efforts, and as such are open to some artistic interpretation. However, after a while, you start getting a very good idea where the envelope "wants to go." It is almost like having a map.

When drawing envelopes, it is important to draw the boundaries parallel to each other. Just recognize that as they turn over, this may be difficult to maintain exactly. Envelopes, when they turn, turn over gradually. It is very important not to treat the initial envelope boundary as a trendline, particularly when it's turning from an uptrend to a downtrend. Rather characteristically, the market will put on a rally attempt within seven trading days of an envelope turn. You have to allow the envelopes enough room to encompass this action. As the market turns, it is

105

by no means uncommon for part of a day's action to fall outside the envelope. The rule here is that the close has to be included within the envelope. It is impossible to draw satisfactorily-looking envelopes if all the market action is included.

Once you have acquired a certain amount of data and also a degree of familiarity with single-width envelopes, double-width envelopes should be attempted. These basically are twice the width of the single-width envelopes and seek to isolate significant turning points. It is important to realize that they seldom share upper or lower envelope boundaries with single-width envelopes for any distance. Double-width envelopes are less precise than single-width envelopes. Nevertheless, they comprise some useful timing signals and provide one of the indicators in the RSL System.

The basic envelope signals are very easy to identify and are usually quite clear cut. The best signals are given on a sharp penetration of the upper envelope boundary on the buy side and the lower envelope boundary on the sell side. Sometimes the market will close almost exactly on one or the other boundary. As a general rule, it is better to give the market the benefit of the doubt on such a day. Mutual fund traders should wait until the last half hour to trade. Things can get quite tricky, as the market can go to an apparent sell only to reverse itself in the last five minutes. Mutual funds usually allow trading up to the 4 p.m. close, so try to postpone the decision as late as possible without risking not getting through to the fund.

Futures contracts often predict trend changes, although not always; i.e., an envelope sell on the futures will often alert the trader to the possibility of a sell the following day on the cash, if one has not already occurred. It is a good idea to keep envelopes on futures for this reason, and of course they have to be kept if you are trading futures using the system. The envelope system buys strength and sells weakness. As such, it cannot ever expect to catch the exact tops or the exact bottoms of a move.

Mutual fund switching using envelope signals may slightly under-perform a buy and hold strategy in a strongly uptrended market, but will give invaluable protection in a down-trended market. Since nobody knows the extent of a move once a change in trend has been identified, it is essential to exit the market on a unit basis when indicated by the envelopes. There is no way for the market to change direction without a change in envelope direction.

The beauty of the envelopes is that they will follow a market for as long as the market is trending in a particular direction. As such, they represent bands above and below centered moving averages of varying time periods, depending on the length of the market move in question. They are, therefore, much more versatile than trying to use moving averages of fixed lengths. With envelopes, *it is impossible to stay on the wrong side of the market for very long.* And you have to force yourself to get right back in if you take a premature exit.

When the envelope changes direction, start the new envelope at an angle equivalent to but opposite from that of the previous envelope. This may have to be revised later as the market action unfolds, but it is the best way I have found to get the new envelope started.

In summary, the envelope system provides a road map of the market with a certain predictive value in that a trend once identified and in effect tends to stay in effect. But the real value in the envelopes lies not in such predictive value, but in the way they follow the market and allow you to get aboard a good move relatively early on. The envelope indicators, both SW and DW, are an essential part of the RSL System.

If you would like more practice with these indicators, I highly recommend you review J.M. Hurst's classic book.

Chapter 6

The Advance/Decline (A/D) Indicator

PRINCIPLE

This indicator is one of the most well-known and well-established market indicators. The idea behind it is that the market cannot advance significantly without having more advancing issues than declining issues. Of course, the market can do so on a short term basis, but such an advance is immediately suspect when not confirmed by market "breadth." In the RSL System, the A/D indicator is used in two ways:

1. As part of the NAT indicator. This is the NY Comp-A/D-Trend combined indicator. This will be fully discussed under the Trend Indicator (TI).
2. As its specialized sub-indicator, a 0.1 exponential MA of the Advance/Decline figures. This is one of the core indicators of the RSL System and is featured in the Master Worksheet. This indicator is always either positive or negative.

TECHNIQUE

Necessary Data

All that has to be done is to accumulate the difference between the advancing issues and the declining issues on a daily basis.

Calculation

In order to avoid negative numbers, it is usual to start the indicator at a significantly positive figure, such as plus 10,000. The actual value is immaterial as the crucial feature is the accumulated ups and downs in the indicator. Back to January 1989 and a starting value of 10,000. Table 14 gives the values. Each day the net number of advancing less declining issues is added to or subtracted from the accumulated figure. The indicator takes no time to stabilize, but clearly will only be of value when a significant amount of data has accumulated. Fortunately, the A/D line, as it is called, is featured regularly in such publications as *Investor's Daily* and *Barron's*. This means that trendline analysis can begin immediately.

ACTION SIGNALS

Buy and sell signals are generated on straightforward trendline breaks similar to those already discussed. The most reliable, of course, are the longest trendlines. The most reliable of all are those that are in consonance with trendline signals from the NY Comp (plotted on a close-only basis) and the Trend Indicator (Chapter 8). Indeed, the triad together form the NAT indicator, to be discussed under the Trend Indicator. Also, in the RSL System, the A/D line, although very important, is not used as a primary indicator. However, its 0.1 exponential MA, which is a specialized sub-indicator, is one of the core values of the system and is entered on the daily master worksheet. It is always on buy or sell.

110

Table 14
ADVANCE-DECLINE LINE

	Advances	Declines	A-D	Starting Value 10,000 A-D Line	0.1 Exp.MA
Jan 3	619	942	− 323	9677	9968
4	1187	331	+ 856	10533	10025
5	837	611	+ 226	10759	10098
6	964	522	+ 442	11201	10208
Jan 9	880	639	+ 241	11442	10331
10	621	816	− 195	11247	10423
11	822	606	+ 216	11463	10527
12	907	586	+ 321	11784	10653
13	836	615	+ 221	12005	10788
Jan 16	695	679	− 34	11971	10906
17	624	800	− 176	11795	10995
18	1036	474	+ 562	12357	11131
19	814	643	+ 171	12528	11271
20	659	755	− 96	12432	11387
Jan 23	553	912	− 359	12073	11456
24	1009	477	+ 532	12605	11571
25	820	648	+ 172	12777	11692
26	962	510	+ 452	13229	11846
27	929	611	+ 318	13547	12016
Jan 30	876	570	+ 306	13853	12200
31	960	541	+ 419	14272	12407

STOPS

These will be discussed under the Trend Indicator.

SPECIALIZED SUB-INDICATORS

There is a very important indicator based on the A/D line. This is the 0.1 exponential MA of the accumulated values (Table 14). The 0.1 exponential MA is run exactly like the 0.15 exponential MA of the NY Comp that we already discussed under the W(D)[10] indicator. The difference, of course, is that the multiplication factor is 0.1 not 0.15. The indicator will take about 20 trading days to stabilize. Buy signals are given when the A/D accumulated figure closes above its 0.1 exponential MA and sell signals when it closes below. It is quite easy to figure out before the close of the trading day what the necessary number will be. In Table 14, the A/D accumulated figure was 14,272 as of January 31 and its 0.1 exponential MA was at 12,407. This means that a sell would only be possible on the close of the next day's trading if there are $12,407 - 14,272 = 1,865$ more declining issues than advancing issues. On October 19, 1987, there was a negative figure of 1,911 more declines than advances so, realistically, a sell would be quite unlikely (but anything can happen).

I have experimented over the years with adding either a fixed number or a certain percent of the net figure to the actual figure obtained in order to reduce whipsaws. Whipsaws are the bane of this particular indicator and make it unsuitable for use as a stand-alone indicator. I finally decided that such a process amounted to optimization and I decided to use the straightforward numbers obtained. The numbers are rounded off to the nearest ten points; i.e., 12,474 and 12,465 are both counted as 12,470.

It is important to note that even a fifty-point addition or subtraction would not have helped a bad period for the indicator, such as that from 12/19/88 through 12/28/88. This period consisted of seven trading days with five trading signals.

I have also over the years experimented with other exponential moving averages, particularly the 0.15 and 0.2. The 0.1 has outperformed these other indicators on backtesting and is capable of some fine trading periods; but like all moving average systems, it may go through choppy periods that make it (and other MA indicators) unsuitable for use as the sole indicator in a system. Fortunately, we avoid this problem in the RSL System as we have eight indicators to choose from.

OVERALL COMMENT AND SUMMARY

The A/D line itself yields useful information about market action and is known by many who know little else about technical analysis. It is the granddaddy of all technical indicators. When working with the MBI, I decided to use the advancing and declining issues as a ratio and to run 10 day MAs of the figures to derive the A/D component of the MBI. This allowed the longer term trend in the numbers to show up well and, in my opinion, resulted in increased reliability. There have been many modifications made to the basic A/D line to increase its usefulness and sensitivity. Colby and Meyers in *"The Encyclopedia of Technical Market Indicators"* [3] list a number of such indicators.

One of the most interesting is "STIX," based on the advancing and declining data. To quote from Colby and Meyers, Page 471, "STIX" is an exponentially smoothed short-term market breadth indicator. It is calculated on a daily basis in two steps, using the NYSE advance/decline data. First, you compute a ratio by dividing the number of advancing issues by the number of advancing issues plus the number of declining issues. That ratio is multiplied by 0.09 and added to the product of the previous day's STIX value multiplied by 0.91. This smoothing approximates a 21-day simple moving average." Low STIX readings are bearish and high STIX readings are bullish.

Jerry Appel, Editor of *"Systems and Forecasts,"* a well-established and well-respected stock market advisory (Signalert

Corporation, 150 Great Neck Road, Great Neck, NY 11021), likes STIX and refers to it quite frequently. I have not used this indicator in my own work, being content with the A/D line as traditionally calculated. But it is clear that some very important market information is to be found in the number of advancing and declining issues.

The 0.1 exponential MA is an important indicator in the RSL System. It will trigger as the RSI climbs above 40, sometimes before and sometimes after the 21/5 indicator. Both these indicators are always either on Buy or on Sell and are important core indicators in the RSL System. We will consider the 21/5 indicator next.

Chapter 7

The 21/5 MA Indicator

PRINCIPLE

Moving averages are well known. The 21/5 indicator represents a simple 21-day MA moved *forward* (offset) by five trading days. This offset feature is used to reduce whipsaws and works quite nicely. The downside, of course, is that the exit point will usually be at a level below that given by the same moving average without the five-day offset. For those owning an Epson QX-10 Computer, part of the original Commodity Quote Graphics TQ 20/20 System, there is some very handy software available from Coast Investment Software, P.O. Box 809, Hermosa Beach, CA 90254 (Joe diNapoli, President). This software has the offset feature available from any period up to 0 to 5 days for any MA up to 140 days. I highly recommend this software, which enables you to enter daily data on the market and which will generate from this data some very clear and valuable charts.

The 21/5 indicator works because markets go into trading periods. The offset feature will reduce whipsaws. Figure 20 gives a simple 21-day moving average with no offset while Figure 21 gives the same MA with a five-day offset. Three costly whipsaws would have been avoided using the offset feature.

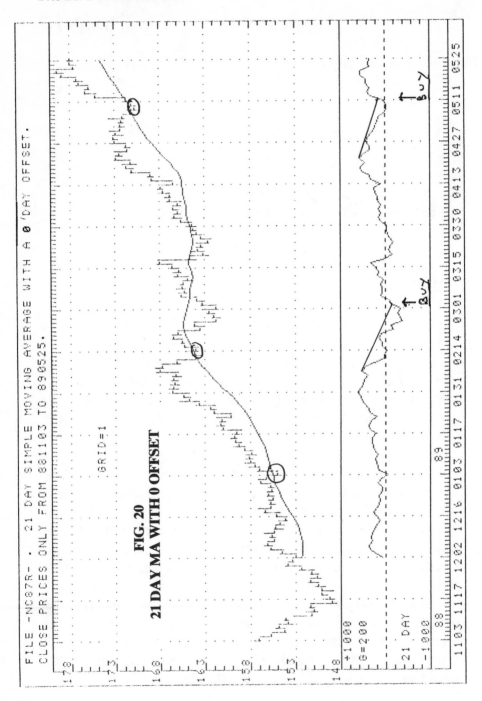

FIG. 20
21 DAY MA WITH 0 OFFSET

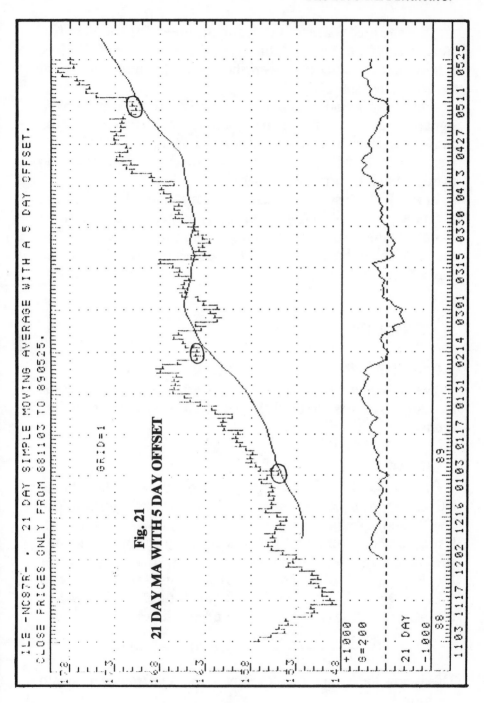

Fig. 21
21 DAY MA WITH 5 DAY OFFSET

117

Another nice feature is that the numbers for the next five trading days will be available from the computer and can be entered on the master daily worksheet. I do this at the top half of the 21/5 box (Table 17).

The 21-day period was chosen for the RSL System because the signals are active enough to avoid serious drawdown but not too active, particularly with a five-day offset feature, to "whipsaw" frequently. All MA indicators have a tendency to whipsaw no matter what time frame is averaged.

In the RSL System, the 21/5 is just one of the indicators available, but it is an important one and gives some excellent signals. If the market can mount a decent rally, it is certain that the 21/5 MA indicator will pick the move up fairly early on and stay with it.

TECHNIQUE

Necessary Data

Twenty-one days of market activity are necessary to start the indicator. There is no stabilizing period as it is a simple moving average.

Calculation

On new Day 1 (= Day 22), the difference between the value of the NY Comp on that day and the old Day 1 (21 days ago) is divided by 21 and the figure applied to the old MA (Table 15). Using the NY Comp values from January again, the 21-day simple moving average on January 31 (trading day 21) was 160.404, the 21-day total divided by 21. This is the trigger level for February 7, five trading days into the future. The 21-day MA for February 1, the new Day 1, is found as follows:

$$\frac{(166.47 - 154.98)}{21} + 160.404 = 160.951$$

This is now the trigger level for February 8, five trading days into the future.

Table 15
21 Day MA OFFSET BY 5 Days (21/5 Indicator)

DAY	1989	NYC
11	Jan 3	154.98
2	4	157.06
3	5	157.49
4	6	157.46
5	9	158.15
6	10	157.85
7	11	158.65
8	12	159.26
9	13	159.58
10	16	159.78
11	17	159.48
12	18	161.01
13	19	161.26
14	20	161.16
15	23	160.13
16	24	161.99
17	25	162.33
18	26	163.60
19	27	164.78
20	30	165.36
21	31	166.63
1	Feb 1	166.47
2	2	166.35
3	3	
4	6	
5	7	
6	8	

21d MA	Offset 5 days		
160.404	1		
160.951	2		
	3		
	4		
	5	160.40	Trigger For Feb 7
	1	160.95	Trigger For Feb 8

119

ACTION SIGNALS

The simplest of all. When the market, as judged by the NY Comp, closes above the trigger level, it is a buy. Remember, the average is offset by five trading days. The sell signal is the reverse. There is no "play" in the system—a 1¢ close above or below the displaced MA triggers the signal. Fortunately, the move will usually be more definite.

STOPS

This is a basic market system, with the indicator always on buy or sell. Since trading mutual funds does not put us into a sell mode, it is, as far as the funds are concerned, a buy and exit-into-cash system.

The 21/5 indicator can be used for trading the S&P or NYFE futures contracts, but I have found a nine-day MA displaced five days (the 9/5 indicator) is better for trading futures. Note that in Figure 13, "The Aberrant Day," a 9/5 MA is shown; and though the Aberrant Day caused a whipsaw, a trader staying with the signals would have made some real money.

SPECIALIZED SUB-INDICATORS

There is one important specialized sub -indicator that is worth knowing about. The idea behind this sub-indicator is similar to the W(D)[10] Indicator. That is, a detrending oscillator (so named by Joe diNapoli) which measures the difference between the market itself and the moving average over the period selected. This is a simple MA, not an exponential MA as used in the W(D)[10]. In this case, it is the 21-day MA. If you study Figures 20 and 21, you will notice an indicator at the bottom of both charts. This indicator is the same on both charts, i.e., it is not displaced when the moving average is. This is the detrending oscillator and as such is a specialized sub-indicator of the 21/5 MA Indicator. I found that basic trendline analysis (Figure 20) works well on this indicator. There will be times when the detrender will set up a W-formation quite similar to the W(D)[10] Indicator for this aspect of market action. The software from Coast Investment Software allows the detrender to be programmed on its own via a program known as COPP. The really nice feature of this program is that it allows the trader to ask "what if" questions, such as:

1. If the market closes at X tomorrow, what will the detrending oscillator value be?
2. If the detrending oscillator has a value of Y tomorrow, where will the market close?

OVERALL COMMENT AND SUMMARY

This is a great indicator. When the market goes into trend mode, the indicator will get you aboard early enough. With the five-day offset feature it will also keep you in during most aberrant days. No indicator is perfect, but this is one of the core indicators in the RSL System, and it is staunch. It is always on buy or sell and as such forms part of the core data for the RSL System.

Chapter 8

The Trend Indicator (TI)

PRINCIPLE

Richard Russell, who edits "Dow Theory Letters," is a well-known market technician and calls one of his proprietary indicators, "The Primary Trend Indicator." Some years ago a good friend of mine, a portfolio manager working in Boston, told me he thought he had worked out what Russell was doing with his primary trend indicator. He may or may not have come close to what Russell actually does, but I have kept the indicator he gave me for many years and have found it very reliable. It is with the title "The Trend Indicator" that I will describe what he told me, in fairness to Richard Russell.

The principle is quite simple. Eight important market indices are assigned a value ranging from $+1$ to -1, with 0 being assigned to any unchanged values. This is done on a daily basis and an accumulated total is calculated. Obviously, as with the A/D line, the market cannot advance without the indicators in the TI becoming positive. The eight indicators used (recognizing Russell may actually be doing something quite different) are:

1. Dow Jones Industrials
2. Dow Jones Transports
3. Dow Jones Utilities
4. Dow Jones 20-Bond Index

5. Advances vs. Declines
6. 15 Most-Active Stocks
7. New Highs vs. New Lows
8. The Standard and Poor's Index Itself

TECHNIQUE

Necessary Data

After the close of each market day, determine the accumulated total for the TI. As stated, each can be $+1$, 0, or -1. The values are unambiguous, although I should stress that when assessing the 15 most-active stocks that only the number of issues advancing vs. the number of those declining should be considered. Unchanged issues should be ignored. There is no stabilization period, although clearly the indicator will only become valuable when a reasonable body of data has been collected.

Calculation

This is simplicity itself. Start with an arbitrary number like 2000 and run a daily accumulated total (very much as the A/D line is run). The indicator is plotted simultaneously with:

1. The NY Comp, plotted on a close-only basis;
2. The A/D line.

The A/D line and the TI are by their nature worked out on a close-only basis. The three values should be plotted underneath each other to form the composite New York Comp, A/D, and TI —or NAT indicator.

ACTION SIGNALS

The idea is that two of the three indicators should confirm each other. Straightforward trendline analysis is used. Figure 22 shows characteristic NAT buy and sell signals. Note that sell signals are also sell short signals for futures traders.

There is also another set of signals based on this composite in-

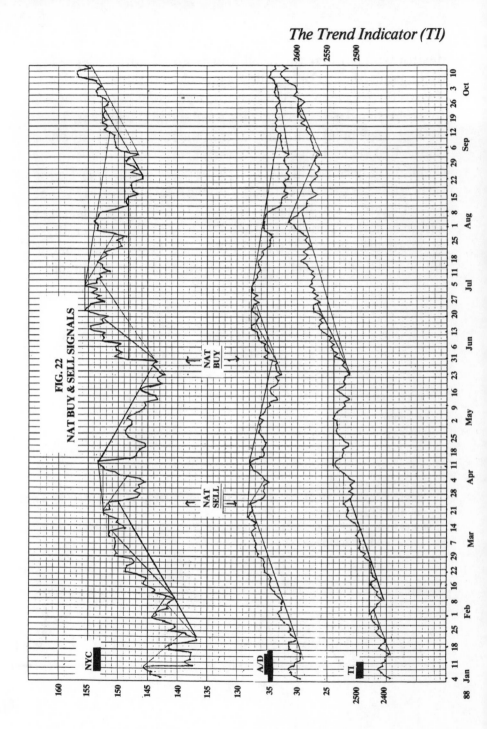

FIG. 22
NAT BUY & SELL SIGNALS

dicator which utilize the break-out from a trading range. The trading range has to be established in each of the three indicators. Two of three have to break-out of the trading range on the upside for a buy signal and vice versa for a sell signal (Figure 23). These trading range break-outs can occur in the RSL System anywhere on the RSI scale; indeed, some very profitable break-out buy signals have occurred in *overbought* territory when, after a good rally, the market has entered a consolidating trading range period. Here again, it may be difficult to force yourself to take action when the market looks "toppy." But under these circumstances, the unit if traded will usually be an additional unit not an initial unit, and any other units will already be profitable.

FIG. 23
NAT TRADING RANGE SIGNALS

Each Component
NY Comp
A/D Line
T1

Has to set up a trading range.
Signal to Buy is given on breakout of the trading range to the upside by 2 out of 3 NAT indicators.
Signal to Sell is given on breakout of the trading range to the downside by 2 out of 3 NAT indicators.

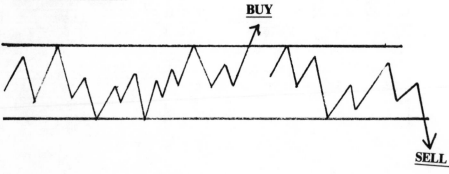

STOPS

These are based on trendline analysis also and again two out of three of the indicators must confirm the signal. The stops are really exit signals, as the RSL System is not designed to go short.

SPECIALIZED SUB-INDICATORS

There is one very reliable specialized sub-indicator based just on the TI. It employs point and figure charting (P&F). P&F charting is an old stock market technique that allows the market some room against the trend. Basically, P&F charting uses boxes of varying sizes. The box is only filled on a rising scale when the highest value in the box is achieved. The values for the box are placed *opposite the spaces between lines, not* the lines themselves. Using the TI and a box width of 5 TI points, the following are the TI values for January 1989 (Table 16). Figure 24 shows standard P&F buy and sell signals.

The standard reversal unit in P&F charting is a three-box reversal. Optimization is possible. The specialized sub-indicator of the TI uses a box width of 5 units and a three-box reversal. This means that under certain circumstances, a three-box reversal can occur on two sharply down days when the market is in an uptrend (or two strong up days when the market is in a downtrend), as the maximum possible total from two TI days is 16 (8 x 2). But a reversal can only occur to the downside when the TI has a value within one TI unit of the bottom of the box. For instance, if the TI value is 2552, a three-box reversal is impossible in two days as the TI can only fall to 2536 on two "– 8" days (i.e., not to the bottom of the box at 2535), which is 15 points below the bottom of the box that relates to 2551. The real point to grasp is that if the accumulated total is, say, 2554 (which is close to but not at the 2555 box) the 2554 value counts as 2550 so that a fall to 2535 is necessary for a three-box reversal; i.e., the reversal is *not* 15 points from the 2554 reading, but 15 points from the bottom of the box which is at 2550.

TABLE 16
Trend Indicator Values in Jan '89

Start With Value Of 2000

Jan 3	−6	1994
4	+6	2000
5	+2	2002
6	+6	2008
Jan 9	+4	2012
10	0	2012
11	+6	2018
12	+7	2025
13	+6	2031
Jan 16	+3	2034
17	+2	2036
18	+8	2044
19	+2	2046
20	−3	2043
Jan 23	−6	2037
24	+8	2045
25	+6	2051
26	+6	2057
27	+6	2063
Jan 30	+6	2069
31	+6	2075

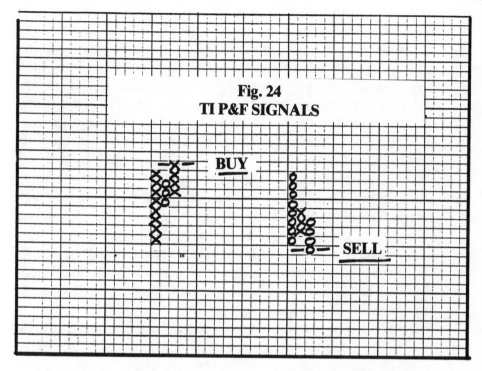

Fig. 24
TI P&F SIGNALS

Convention uses Xs for rising values and 0s when the column changes to down values on a three-box reversal.

Three-box reversals are not primary signals on the P&F specialized sub-indicator. The primary signals follow standard P&F charting techniques (Figure 24).

There are other P&F buy and sell formations, but these two are the only ones I use in the RSL System. However, be assured that some magnificant market moves have been signaled by a standard P&F buy on the TI (as for instance occurred in August 1982).

OVERALL COMMENT AND SUMMARY

The TI is really part of a composite indicator formed with the

New York Comp, plotted on a close-only basis, and the A/D line to give the NAT Indicator. But divergence between the action of the indicators will give important clues to subsequent market action, as happened before the October 1987 crash. The NAT sell was in place by Aug 28 (Figure 25). Figure 25 also shows how the A/D line set up a negative divergence with the New York Comp in late September 1987, certainly a sufficient warning. But note also that the TI line, normally somewhat stronger than the A/D line, behaved in terrible fashion. Using the component NAT indicators, severe doubts about the market should have been in place around October 5, 1987 when the market made a new high *not* confirmed by either the N. Y. Comp or the TI. A total exit was definitely in order by October 14, when the lows of July 23 were violated. Anyone closely following the market and trading mutual funds should have been out 100% by October 14 if not significantly before. The absolute last chance was Oct. 15, when the July 1 low was taken out (Figure 25).

I realize that portfolio managers and others committed to individual common stocks do not have the luxury of being able to liquidate their positions on a dime, that is, a telephone call. Which is why anyone following the RSL System should be able to beat not only the money managers, but many market letter writers as well. Mark Hulbert, editor of the Hulbert Financial Digest (HFD),[*] has not endeared himself to all market letter writers by holding up to them the non-warped reflection of the performance of their recommendations. His methodology is explained with great care and is universally applied. In the June 1989, Volume XI, Number 10 edition of the HFD, he published a list of the top performing newsletters from the August 31, 1987 high through May 31, 1989. He follows (I believe) 111 newsletters. The top spot went to "Switch Fund Timing" with a gain of 37.27%. However, I came in #14 of 111 for my managed accounts (though, of course, I was not actually listed as I do not publish a newsletter). I had a gain of 12.65%.

There is a significant difference between 37.27% and 12.65%, I grant you; but it is important to realize that the average equity mutual fund took about 18 months just to get back to even with

[*] HFD, 316 Commerce St., Alexandria, VA 22314

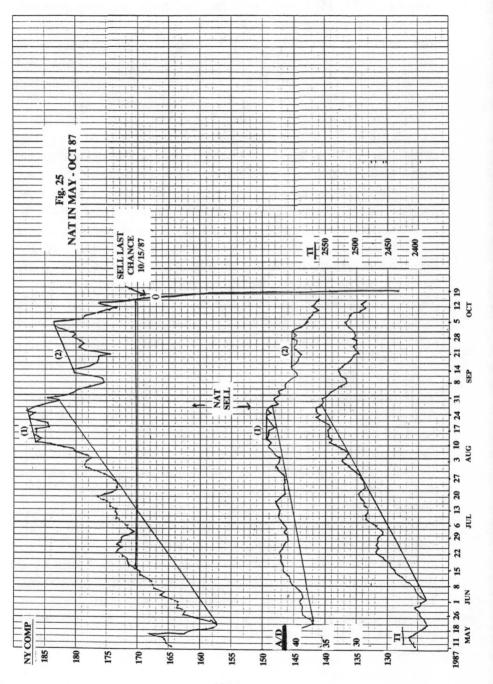

the August 31, 1987 high, and this is with dividends re-invested. The Dow during this period was down 0.81%, although the S&P did somewhat better, being up 3.41%. Also, I have been more cautious since the crash with the money I manage. I have not wanted to involve more than two units of managed money in equity funds. Had I gone with the full RSL four-unit system, it is clear that my performance would have been better. I will never forget the look on the face of one of the members of the group whose money I manage when late in the afternoon on October 19, 1987, with the market down 500 points or so, he asked me if we were still in the market. It was my reply that triggered his beatific expression. I told him we had been 100% in cash since October 8.

I had no way of knowing—and I never try to predict—that a crash of such magnitude was in the wings. I was out because the indicators said out, it was that simple. And that is really all there is to following a system. Just take the signals and to hell with one's own ideas about what the market "should" do. It will always try to embarrass the greatest number of those who hold such opinions. Flying by the seat of your pants may be O.K. for WWI pilots, but has nothing to do with any long-term success in the market.

Mutual fund switching can only be activated during the day; and whether the order is in early or late, provided the order is received before the end of trading, the price is the same. This is a frustration on strongly up or down days, but it also means the trader has just one decision to make; and that he can postpone that decision until the end of the trading day. He does not have to watch the market very closely during the entire day. He can catch up with it in the afternoon. Such a trading pattern is fully compatible with a regular job outside the market.

But I believe anyone trying to day-trade futures should have access during the entire trading day to good market information. I know that there are "set-it and forget-it" day trading systems out there. Vilar Kelly runs a successful hot-line using just such a system (Vilar Kelly, 56 Brittania Drive, Danbury, CT, 06841).

Anyone wanting to day-trade futures and keep a regular job should look into Vilar's service, which has an excellent track record.

For a time I had a Commodity Quote Graphics TQ 20/20 System with a satellite dish at my home. This is a marvelous system, but I promise it is easier to go out to work at a regular job than it is to try day-trading for a profit unless you are very skilled. The machine will dominate your trading day. A breakout can occur at anytime and Mary, my wife, to whom this book is dedicated, would notice that the breakout would nearly always occur at those times when she was picking up the children or the groceries or running other errands. I tried it on a week's vacation, trading on a daily basis. The markets open at 9:30. By 11:30 on a quiet day, I was bored and as often as not frustrated. There is no doubt that standard technical analysis works on *all* time frames. The problem with a "dish"—instant quote system—is that the 15-minute time frame seems like forever when watching the screen. Inevitably, your trading time frame gets shorter and shorter.

Let me tell you, short-term intraday trading is stressful. All trading is stressful, but I feel a lot happier trading mutual funds and not having to watch the market on a tick-by-tick basis.

I recognize there are a few hardy souls out there. Larry Williams is clearly one, who can not only take the stress but thrive upon it. But my advice, offered at no extra charge, to anyone contemplating quitting the old boring 9 to 5 Dolly Parton routine to amass a fortune by trading at home is to forget it. The only real money is made by position trading and that does not require anyone to sit "bug-eyed" watching the machine "squiggles." I feel I know now what to do to be a successful day trader. But I cannot stand the mixture of anticipation and boredom. Win, lose, or draw, trading the RSL System, you know that during the course of any trading day, there is only one decision to be made and that, believe me, is a bonus. Also, it doesn't require any expensive equipment. The necessary data is there on Financial News Network (FNN, a great network) at nominal cost. Money can be made using the RSL System, believe me. And you do not have to quit your job to do so. It is certain that the signals work for mutual funds, and they also work for futures contracts based on the general market such as the S&P 500 and the NYFE. I know nothing about trading soybeans or feeder cattle, but it is clear that any system that is successful trading the general stock market has to be successful in trading futures contracts based on the same market (providing the same signals and stops are used). In Chapter 9, we will examine this concept in more detail.

The RSL System In Action

We will consider the NY Comp as a substitute for trading in individual mutual funds and will follow the RSL signals as they occurred during the decline in October, 1988 (not 1987). On October 21, 1988 the NY Comp topped out at 159.42, falling by November 17th to a value of 149.24, a 6.39% loss. This put all the RSL indicators on sell, so this is a good time to see how the system works after a decline of some magnitude. On November 17th the RSI value was 35 and the MBI value 41, so both were oversold. The 0.1 A/D indicator had gone on sell on October 27 and the 21/5 on November 4. The other RSL indicators were also on sell, so the B-S column on the master work sheet was in solidly negative territory (− 8). The trend was clearly down (Figure 26). Our old friend the MBI had fallen below 45 and the RSI was also oversold (Figure 11). This is the time to expect a rally to commence, but not to act before the signals say so.

There is also something interesting going on with the W(D)[10] indicator. The values for the week of November 7th were as follows: − 2.18, − 1.38, − 1.96, − 1.52, and − 3.71. The value of − 3.71 had certainly passed the − 2.00 level necessary for a valid formation. The values for the week of November 14 were − 3.32, − 2.58, − 3.88, − 3.39, and − 2.08. The W has formed and any upside action will be a buy signal (Figure 16 shows the formation

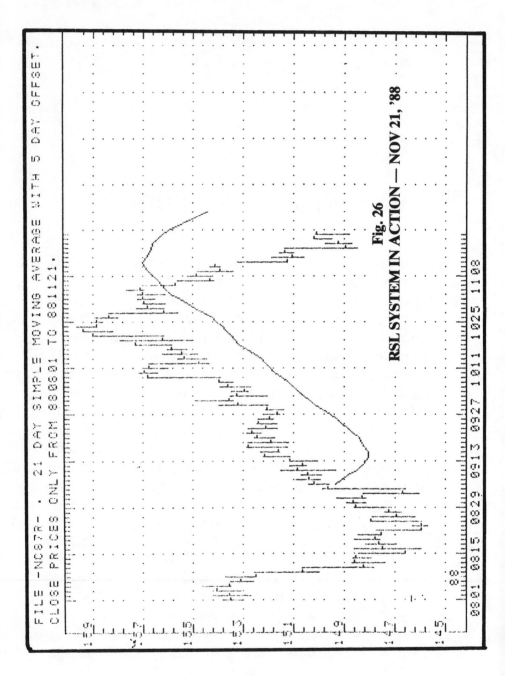

Fig. 26

RSL SYSTEM IN ACTION — NOV 21, '88

nicely). What happens? On Monday, November 21 the market closes up 3.6 points on the Dow, though the NY Comp is down from 150.18 to 150.10. However, the W(D)^{10} indicator rises to -1.84, taking out the middle limb of the W and so giving a buy signal. The reading on Nov. 18 took out the -2.58 reading of Nov. 15 but was still below -2.00. In such a situation it is safer to wait for a reading less than -2.00.

The RSI also gives a standard buy signal on a similar bottoming formation (Figure 11). Not only that, but it is clear that the MBI is about to go on buy with a close above 45. Note that while an idea of the closing RSI value can easily be projected by the value of the Dow shortly before the close of a trading day, the MBI is more complicated to predict since three different indicators are involved. The final signal, unless the market is strongly up or down, will usually apply to the following trading day (see Table 17).

What should be done? If we assign $10,000 to each unit, for a total of $40,000, two units should be bought with the NY Comp at 150.10, giving us a total of 133.24 "shares" of the NY Comp. ($20,000 divided by 150.10 = 133.24). Note that the W(D)^{10} signal clearly seen in Figure 16 will usually trigger before the other indicators, so the present situation is a little unusual. As an aside, I apologize for having to use several different charts and tables. But with eight main indicators to choose from, it is impossible to show them all on the same chart successfully.

On the next day, November 22, the MBI 45 crossing to the upside is confirmed with the MBI closing at 47. This becomes apparent after running the previous day's number, so an MBI buy signal is in effect. Before the close of November 22 it is clear that the SW envelope will also go on buy with a close above the signal level of 150.00 (Figure 16). Should two additional units be bought, or just one? My trading style is to go with one additional unit, so a third unit is bought giving an additional 66.42 shares for a total of 199.66 shares. Three out of the four possible units are now working. It is unusual to get four valid signals, and we have taken three of them, quickly even though the market is still

Table 17
RSL SYSTEM
Master Work Sheet
(Nov '88 Rally)

'88	New Buy Signals		Total Buy	NYC	RSI	MBI	21/5	0.1A/D	New Sell Signals	Total Sell	Net B-S
Nov 17			0	149.24	35	41	156.49			8	−8
				150.18	38	41	156.40				
Nov 21	W(D)[10]	RSI	2	150.10	39	47	156.19			6	−4
22	SW	MBI	4	150.55	43	46	155.97			4	0
23				151.41	47	50	155.57				
24	THANKSGIVING										
25				150.63	43	49	155.24				
Nov 28	NAT		5	151.75	45	55	154.82			3	+2
29	DW	(MBI)	6	152.43	50	58	154.38			2	+4
30				153.90	54	61	153.98				
Dec 1				153.37	50	65	153.63				
2				153.02	48	65	153.26				
5	21/5		7	154.48	56	65	153.03 +		(21/5 on B)	1	+6
6	0.1A/D		8	155.78	61	68	152.82	+		0	+8
7				156.48	62	68	152.67				
8			7	155.37	58	65	152.50	−	0.1A/D	1	+6
9	0.1A/D		8	155.59	58	65	152.31	+		0	+8
Dec 12			7	155.34	57	64	152.19	−	0.1A/D	1	+6
13			6	155.24	58	61	152.19		SW	2	+4
14				154.73	55	57	152.28				
15				154.17	54	56	152.31				
16	SW		7	155.16	59	61	152.39			1	+6
Dec 19	0.1A/D		8	156.38	65	60	152.45	+		0	+8
20			7	155.74	62	58	152.64	−	0.1A/D	1	+6
21			6	155.73	61	56	152.81		SW	2	+4
22				155.50	60	59	152.95				
23	SW	0.1A/D	8	156.06	62	59	153.24	+		0	+8
Dec 26	CHRISTMAS VACATION DAY										
27			7	155.58	59	59	153.58	−	0.1A/D	1	+6
28	0.1A/D		8	155.81	60	62	153.85	+		0	+8
29				156.26	65	65	154.12				

not clearly uptrended. But remember, there is no point in keeping indicators unless they are followed. At this point I like to wait for one of the slower indicators to trigger before putting the final unit down. My personal preference is to wait in this situation for either the 21/5 or the 0.1 A/D to trigger. It must be noted that a valid NAT signal was given on November 28, and both a DW envelope signal and an MBI trendline break signal were given on November 29 (Figures 16 and 11 respectively). Since the MBI trendline break signal is not a specialized sub-indicator signal it does not increase the number of buy signals, which is why it is in parentheses on the master work sheet.

There is no doubt that the market wants to go higher. What happens? The 21/5 indicator gives a strong buy on December 5 (Figure 27), a day the market is up 31.5 points on the Dow. The RSI rises from 48 to 56 on this move, still in mid-range. The MBI closes at 65, which is close to overbought, but remember this indicator tops out ahead of the market. The fourth unit is now engaged at a price for the NY Comp of 154.48. 64.73 additional shares are acquired for a total four unit commitment of 264.39 shares bought at an average cost of 151.29. The net B/S column is a solid +6. At this point there is nothing to be done but wait. It is impossible to put any more money down, as the total stake is now riding.

An interesting problem arises on December 13 when the SW envelope goes on sell (Figure 16). Also, during the five days before this signal the 0.1 A/D has been whipping back and forth. The NY Comp on December 13 closed at 155.24, just below the trigger to roll over. But the DW envelope (which went on buy November 29—giving a signal we decided not to take as we already had three units working) is clearly uptrended (Figure 16) and the bottom of the DW envelope can now be projected with a good deal of accuracy. It is clear that the Comp can decline to a level around 153.50 without violating the DW envelope.

Futures traders will probably want to take any SW envelope signals when trading futures using the envelopes. Mutual Fund traders should wait to use the DW envelope signal if the 21/5

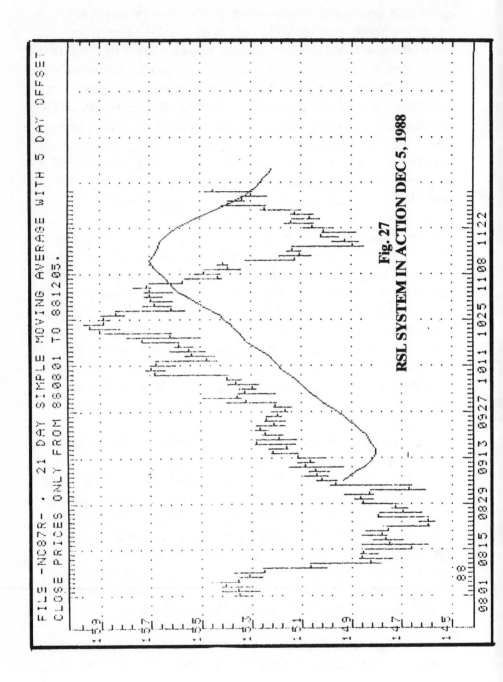

Fig. 27

RSL SYSTEM IN ACTION DEC 5, 1988

signal is on buy. It is usually better for Mutual Fund traders to give the market the benefit of the doubt, but *not* the benefit of a DW envelope sell (it was the DW envelope sell that took me out of the market before the October, 1987 crash (Figure 30)).

Everything else is solidly on buy and the $W(D)^{10}$ indicator is a long way from generating a sell. We have four units riding and decide to stay with the DW envelope signal. The market, with a bit of backing and filling, continues to work its way higher. However, on January 3, 1989, the market closes at 154.98, down 24 points on the Dow. This triggers an RSI sell (Figure 11). Remember we use the Dow for calculating the RSI, so one of the original units bought on November 21 at 150.10 is sold. The profit is $325.00 on $10,000. We are now back to three units.

But on January 12, 1989 a perfect nesting envelope signal already examined in Chapter 5 is given. We re-enter the market at 158.65 using $10,325 as our unit. This gives us 65.08 more shares for a new total of 262.85 shares as follows:

One unit on $W(D)^{10}$ signal at 150.10	= 66.62 shares.
One unit on SW envelope signal at 150.55	= 66.42 shares.
One unit on 21/5 signal at 154.48	= 64.73 shares.
One unit on nesting signal at 158.65	= 65.08 shares.
	262.85

Note: Whenever a unit is exited for profit or loss the exit price becomes the new unit available for the next valid signal *of any type.*

The market now mounts a good rally (note how the 5-day offset feature saves the day in early January) (Figure 28). The exit signals are as follows: Three units on February 9 with a Comp at 166.13. The signals are clear cut. 1) a single width envelope signal which we will take after a rally of this magnitude and a straight up period on the SW envelope. Use the SW not the DW signal afer such a rally. 2) the nesting envelope signal, which always triggers with the SW envelope signal. 3) the $W(D)^{10}$ indicator

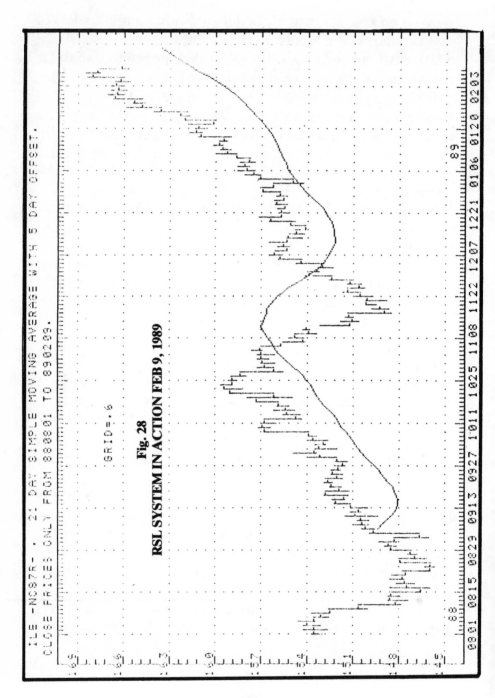

Fig. 28
RSL SYSTEM IN ACTION FEB 9, 1989

142

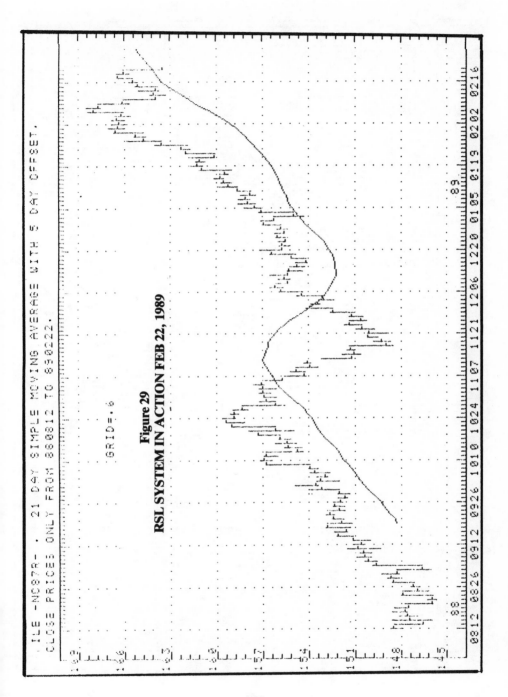

Figure 29
RSL SYSTEM IN ACTION FEB 22, 1989

143

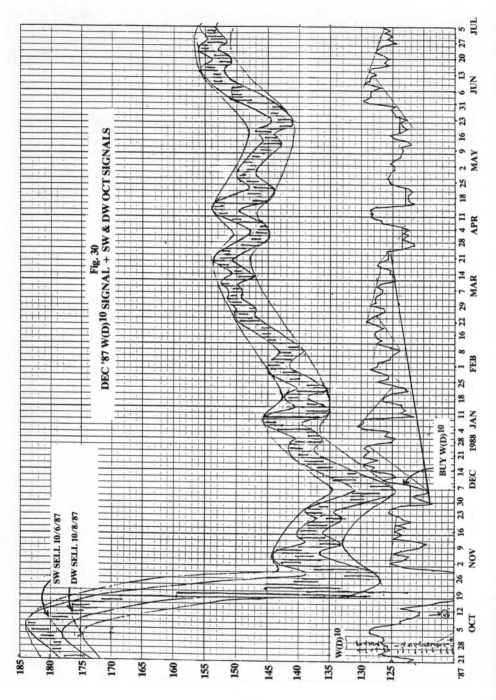

Fig. 30
DEC '87 W(D)^{10} SIGNAL + SW & DW OCT SIGNALS

144

which fell below the 10° (Figures 16 and 28). The total profit was:

1. $1,034.00
2. $ 812.00
3. $1,068.00
   $2,914.00

Note: This is our total realized profit to this date, as the $325.00 made on the first trade was reinvested.

We now have a single unit based on the 21/5 indicator riding. This triggers on February 22 (Figure 29 with the Comp at 163.55). The profit is $587.00. We now exit the market for a total profit of $3,501.00 on $40,000 in roughly 13 weeks (64 trading days). The per cent return is 8.75%, which is quite respectable. Annualized this would be 35.0%, but it is clear that such an annualized figure is not achievable in real-time trading because of the market's inevitable down action. Note that I have not included any profit made while in Money Market Funds for the three units exited February 9. What I wanted to show was how the RSL System can catch a good proportion of the profit to be made on a significant rally. I know that if all four units had been put down on the original W(D)[10] signal and exited on February 9 when the 10° angle was crossed the profits would have been $4,272. But my contention is that the RSL fold-in approach offers significant protection while securing a good profit.

Table 17 will show the action on the master daily work sheet from November 17 through December 29. Notice how the discipline necessary for keeping the eight core indicators up-to-date forces you to stay close to the market. If the RSL System is used as just described, it is not possible to miss a good rally (unless of course you fail to take the signals). If the rally aborts, a full position will not have been established and the damage, if any, will be minor. Entering the market at the absolute bottom of the move just examined and exiting at the absolute top (on a closing basis which is all that is available for Mutual Fund traders) would have yielded a profit of $5,118.00. The RSL system garnered $3,501.00 or 68.4% of the total profit available from the move. Frankly, this is excellent performance, as it is clear no one should attempt to or can buy at the exact bottom or sell at the exact top of a move.

It is important to realize that similar results will be obtained any time there is a good rally in the market. As an example, the rally off the December '87 lows gave a $W(D)^{10}$ signal on December 8 with the NY Comp at 131.42. The 10° exit signal was on March 24, 1988 with the NY Comp at 149.00 (Figure 30). This is a gain of 13.4%. An aggressive trader might ask "Why not use the $W(D)^{10}$ indicator and forget the others?" The answer is that the W formation doesn't always form, so reliance on this as a single indicator may miss a good move. Also, putting the whole bet down on one indicator is more damaging to one's equity when that indicator fails than using the RSL fold-in approach. I grant you that the $W(D)^{10}$ indicator doesn't fail very often, but when it does (as it did early and in late April, 1988) the results are costly.

The choice, of course, is individual. Anyone putting down more than one unit on the $W(D)^{10}$ buy signal, *if one occurs,* will usually outperform those going with only one unit when the signal is a good one. But the point is that every trader must develop a personal interaction with the market. The object of the RSL System is to describe some very successful indicators and how I have used them. I like to have several arrows in my quiver and over the years this approach has stood me in good stead. I think the real trick is to assess the degree of risk with which you feel comfortable. There is a difference between feeling uncomfortable with a particular trade because of your almost always misplaced feelings about the market (we have discussed this feeling at length) and discomfort with the *size* of the position. The RSL System provides a good cushion against the latter form of discomfort, while encouraging the trader to embrace the former. I am old and not very bold—but I am still around.

There is a useful legal concept that states "The thing speaks for itself." "Res Ipsa Loquitur." I believe that a study of the figures and tables that I have presented will convince you that they really do work. While this is primarily a book about mutual switch fund trading, I am aware that there are many aggressive futures traders out there who can pick up some useful ideas from this book (trading in futures and options is discussed in the next chapter). I have to record that although I have not had any experience trading anything but stocks, options, and futures based on general stock market parameters, I don't see why the indicators presented here, such as the RSI-SI, should not work in other markets. Also it is certain that envelopes can be drawn for any market.

Finally, it is important to re-emphasize that all the RSL Indicators can be supplied data for the following market day on a "what if" basis. We have seen that this is more complicated for the MBI (because this is a combination indicator) than for the others, but it certainly can be done. You should note the levels necessary to trigger the indicators *before the market opens*. In this way, a calm nonemotional decision about what should be done can be made before the market has had a chance to affect your emotions and judgement. I believe in writing it all down so that there is a solid basis for action. As an example of what I mean, here are market strategy summaries for the first six trading days of January 1990, ending January 9, 1990, when the RSL System went flat the market.

On the last trading day of 1989, the RSL System had two units in action. Unit #1 should have been entered on a SW envelope signal on December 22, 1989 (the 21/5 also triggered). Remember, signals should be taken 10-15 minutes before the close of the trading day in order to get the closing price of that day. The RSL System called for placing Unit #2 in action on December 28, 1989 on the DW envelope signal (the 0.1 A/D having triggered the day before). The RSI on December 28, 1989 was 62, approaching overbought, but certainly not a contra-indication to the trade (and don't forget RSI-SI. January is a favorite month for this indicator).

MARKET STRATEGY SUMMARY (MSS)
FOR TUESDAY, JANUARY 2, 1990

(Note the first two sections should be completed *before* the market opens on January 2, 1990. The last section details what the market actually did, any comments on the market, and any action taken).

INDICATORS

RSI	62	On Buy (B) but getting overbought. No Sell (S) in the offing.
MBI	58	On B, plenty of room on the upside. No S in the offing.
W(D)^{10}		Did not form.
SW		S on close below 193.50.
DW		S on close below 192.00.
21/5		S on close below 192.12.
0.1 A/D		1260 NET declines needed for S.
NAT		Will only trigger on a market fall of at least 2% (55 points on Dow, 3.90 on NY COMP). *Note:* There is a NAT B signal on a trading range breakout with close above 195.00.
DECISIONS		S seems unlikely. B one unit on close above 195.00.
MARKET ACTION		Market up 57.0 points on the Dow on unimpressive volume. NY COMP closed at 198.00. Program trading probably responsible for much of the action.
		On additional unit bought on NAT breakout.

MSS FOR WEDNESDAY, JANUARY 3, 1990

INDICATORS

RSI	71	In position to generate an RSI-SI B signal on an advance of at least 22 Dow points.
MBI	64	Moving up to overbought. MBI usually tops out ahead of market.
W(D)^{10}		Did not form.
SW		S on close below 194.50.
DW		S on close below 192.50.
21/5		S on close below 192.19.
0.1 A/D		1900 NET declines needed for S.
NAT		Will only trigger on a market fall of at least 3% (85 points on Dow, 5.95 on NY COMP).
DECISIONS		S quite unlikely. B on Dow gain of 22 points or more.
MARKET ACTION		Disappointing lack of follow-through from yesterday's big up day. Not a good sign at this time of year. Dow down 0.5 points. NY COMP closed at 197.80. The RSI-SI trigger level was found by assuming varying advances on the Dow and finding the number of points necessary to reach RSI 74.

MSS FOR THURSDAY, JANUARY 4, 1990

INDICATORS

RSI	71	RSI-SI B still possible.
MBI	70	Any S is a long way off and would need a major disaster.
W(D)^{10}		Did not form.
SW		S on close below 195.50.
DW		S on close below 193.00.
21/5		S on close below 193.2?.
0.1 A/D		1850 NET declines needed for S.
NAT		Same as 1/3/90.
DECISIONS		S still unlikely. B on Dow gain of 22 points or more.
MARKET ACTION		Dow down 13.6 points. NY COMP down 1.53 to close at 196.27. Market not acting at all well. It will have to get on its horse very soon or we will be getting some sell signals.

MSS FOR FRIDAY, JANUARY 5, 1990

INDICATORS

RSI	66	RSI-SI B now impossible.
MBI	70	No change. Same as 1/4/90.
W(D)10		Did not form.
SW		S on close below 196.50.
DW		S on close below 193.50.
21/5		S on close below 192.37.
0.1 A/D		1410 NET declines needed for S.
NAT		S on close below 193.00 if 1100 net declines.

DECISIONS   Market looking very insecure. Early January traditionally strong. Although it is usually wise to allow DW envelope to trigger a S following a SW envelope B signal, the present market action with poor breadth and no follow-through means S one unit if market closes below 196.50, the SW envelope signal S point.

MARKET ACTION   Definite downside action. Dow down 22.8 points. NY COMP down 1.63 to close at 194.64.

One unit sold on SW S signal.

MSS FOR MONDAY, JANUARY 8, 1990

INDICATORS

RSI	60	Will need an upday to set up a S on subsequent weakness.
MBI	67	A decline to 191.50 would now trigger a sell.
W(D)^{10}		Did not form.
SW		On S. Re-entry B at 198.00.
DW		S on close below 194.00.
21/5		S on close below 192.60.
0.1 A/D		960 NET declines needed for S.
NAT		S on close below 193.00 with at least 800 net declines.
DECISIONS		Re-entry B at 198.00. I consider this unlikely given the recent market action. S one unit on DW envelope signal at 194.00.
MARKET ACTION		Dow up 21.1 points. NY COMP closed at 195.33. No action taken.

MSS FOR TUESDAY, JANUARY 9, 1990

INDICATORS

RSI	64	S will need a decline of at least 15 Dow points.
MBI	66	Definite topping action in time with market (a bad sign). S still needs a strongly down day to at least 192.00.
W(D)^{10}		Did not form.
SW		On S. Re-entry B at 197.00.
DW		S on close below 194.50.
21/5		S on close below 192.92.
0.1 A/D		950 NET declines needed for S.
NAT		S on close below 193.50 with at least 800 net declines or TI-8.
DECISIONS		Re-entry B now quite unlikely. S one unit on DW envelope signal. S the last unit if the NAT or RSI also triggers.
MARKET ACTION		Dow down another 28.4 points. NY COMP closed at 193.35.

2 units sold; 1 on DW signal; 1 on RSI signal. Net declines on the NAT indicator were 394. TI was down 6. The NAT did not trigger, but the RSI did. *We are now flat the market.*

There are some points worth emphasizing:

1. These are RSL System signals "by the book." As sometimes happens, I got tied up at work just before 4:00 P.M.
   on January 9. So in actual trading, I did not exit the market
   until Wednesday, January 10. On that day, three additional
   RSL indicators triggered—21/5, 0.1 A/D, and NAT—
   giving a net −4 figure. Do not hang around under these circumstances.

2. Although it was to some extent a value judgment, the decision to take an SW envelope S signal was made in view of
   the action of the market and the other indicators.

3. The SW envelope signal often increases by about $1.00 per
   day and the DW envelope signal by about 0.50¢ (on the NY
   COMP). The actual amounts will vary with the pitch of the
   envelopes.

4, The NET figures necessary for a signal on the 0.1 A/D will
   differ from the net figures on the A/D component in the NAT
   indicator. The 0.1 A/D is an exponential moving average
   while the A/D component is just cumulative and signals are
   given on trendline breaks.

5. Using the NY COMP as a surrogate for individual mutual
   funds, the results would have been as follows (one unit =
   $10,000):

BUY	NY COMP	SELL	NY COMP	+/−
12/22/89	191.95	1/5/90	194.64	+2.69
12/28/89	193.59	1/9/90	193.35	−0.24
1/ 2/90	198.00	1/9/90	193.35	−4.65
				−2.20

This is a loss of $2.20 on three units bought at a total price
583.54 and sold at a total price of 581.34, a loss of 0.38%.

The actual loss in cash would have been $114 on $30,000. This is an acceptable loss given the way the market behaved after the breakout buy on January 2, 1990. Certainly, even exiting on January 10 would have prevented the significant loss waiting in the wings on Friday, January 12 when the market got clobbered by program trading for a 71.5 point loss on the Dow and a 4.46 loss on the NY COMP.*

6. Interestingly, trading in actual mutual funds not the NY COMP, and using the same signals, could have yielded a profit (obviously, this will vary with the fund). Fidelity Trend, one of Fidelity's remaining no-load funds, gave the following results using the same $10,000 unit:

BUY	FIDELITY TREND	SELL	FIDELITY TREND	+/−
12/22/89	43.15	1/5/90	44.50	+1.35
12/28/89	43.67	1/9/90	44.15	+0.48
1/ 2/90	44.84	1/9/90	44.15	−0.69
				+1.14

This works out to a gain of $268.90, or a 0.9% profit on $30,000 over the course of eleven trading days with 3 units in action for only six trading days.

7. The point, however, is still well taken. You have to be prepared for and be able to accept losses. They are inevitable. Using the RSL System, losses should be small. Indeed significantly smaller than the gains, with the proviso, of course, that a crunching bear market will make any long-side gain difficult. But in such a market, not all units will get down on the table and the action of the indicators will warn the trader to stand aside or go short. In a bear market, the indicators behave as follows:

*Note: COMP fell to 179.35 after this (2/23/90)

155

1. RSI and MBI parameters of overbought and oversold drop by approximately 7%.
2. MBI starts topping out *with* not *ahead* of the market.
3. 21/5 and 0.1 A/D indicators spend more time on sell signals than on buy signals.
4. The DW envelope spends more time downstrended than up-trended.
5. NAT shows lower highs and lower lows.

It is difficult, if not impossible, to recognize an underlying change in market climate at its inception. But careful analysis of the indicators will not allow the change to go undetected for long.

AN ALTERNATE APPROACH USING THE RSL SYSTEM INDICATORS:

Some investors prefer an all-or-none approach. Curtis Hesler of *"Professional Timing Service"* is one. For him and others, the *Any 3 RSL System* should be useful. The rules are simple:

Buy

Buy whenever any 3 of the 8 RSL indicators go on buy and appear in the left-hand columns of the daily worksheet. Three indicators *newly* arrived in the left-hand column are needed *triggering within 3 trading days of each other.*

Sell

Sell whenever any 3 of the 8 RSL indicators go on sell and appear in the right-hand columns of the daily worksheet. 3 indicators *newly* arrived in the right-hand column are needed *triggering within 3 trading days of each other.*

Here are the results from 12/27/89 through 7/20/90 using a $10,000 investment in the New York COMP as a substitute for mutual funds. The number of shares to purchase is obtained by dividing the closing price of the New York COMP into the cash available.

ANY 3 RSL SYSTEM

Buy			Sell		
DATE	N.Y. COMP	# "SHARES"	DATE	N.Y. COMP	EQUITY
12/27/89	192.69	51.897	1/ 9/90	193.35	10,034.25
1/31/90	181.50	55.285	2/20/90	181.37	10,027.06
2/28/90	183.07	54.772	3/21/90	186.82	10,232.46
3/27/90	187.40	54.602	4/19/90	185.57	10,132.53
5/ 1/90	182.22	55.606	6/ 8/90	196.05	10,901.56
6/29/90	195.48	55.768	7/20/90	197.68	11,024.25

This is a 10.24% return in seven months as opposed to a buy (12/27/89) and hold approach which during the same period would have yielded a 2.59% return. Also the sell on 7/20/90 got the account safely into cash before the Iraqis invaded Kuwait.

Chapter 10

Trading Futures and Options With The RSL Indicators

The RSL System grew out of my experience with mutual fund trading and a desire to avoid an all-or-none switching approach. It is obvious, just by looking at the charts, that the signals should work for trading vehicles based on the same underlying indices. But even if the signals work, are they of use in *actual trading* or are the drawdowns because of the great leverage involved in the futures market just too large?

If I have $10,000 in a mutual fund which falls 5%, I am out $500 if I close out the trade. But if I use the equivalent $10,000 as margin for only one New York Futures Exchange (NYFE) contract (theoretically such a sum could margin two contracts), I am now trading in a vehicle that has a 500 × multiplier. If the contract falls $1.00, that is the equivalent of $500. So, if the NYFE contract is, say, trading at 190 and it falls 5% to 180.5, the trading loss will be 9.5 (190 − 180.5) × 500 = $4750. This is 47.5% of the original capital. Leverage is a two-edged weapon, and the degree of leverage involved in trading stock index futures contracts makes trading them much more difficult than trading mutual funds.

Note also that options based on futures contracts also have a multiplier of 500 (to be distinguished from the S&P 100 OEX options which trade × 100).

In order to develop a trading system for futures and options based on the RSL indicators, I have made some assumptions which can, of course, be modified. These were:

1. Futures (and options) would be traded on an all or none basis; that is, only one futures contract will be traded, backed by sufficient capital to withstand significant drawdowns. I do not believe the average commodity trader has sufficient capital for multiple contracts and a fold-in approach. Also, the NYFE rather than the S&P contract would be studied as the margin requirements are less.

2. The signals would be taken off the cash indices, not the futures themselves. The reasoning behind this was as follows: Futures can move rapidly from premium over cash to discount to cash and show more volatility because of this. This volatility may disrupt a trend temporarily—the aberrant day.

3. An attempt would be made to find the most profitable combination of signals with the fewest switches (to reduce commission costs and slippage).

4. 15¢ ($75) would be deducted from all round trips for commission costs and slippage. Since all trades would be *close only* trades, such a figure seemed reasonable.

5. No stops would be used in testing the individual indicators for either long or short signals.

6. The trading period tested would coincide at its inception with the period discussed in the main text for mutual fund trading, namely November 1988. The period would end at the end of October 1989, giving close to a year's results.

The results of testing the individual indicators were as follows: (Note all trades are hypothetical. No actual trades based on these indicators were made during this trading period).

160

1. RSI

The RSI did not do very well as a stand-alone indicator. As might be expected in a period of generally rising prices, the long signals fared much better than the short signals. The results were as follows:

LONG		ROLLOVER		SHORT		PROFIT	
		Dec	Mar			Long	Short
Nov 21	150.50	154.15/	155.95	Jan 23	161.00	+ 8.70	
Jan 26	165.05				161.00		− 4.05
	165.05			Feb 9	167.25	+ 2.20	
Mar 7	165.75	Mar	Jun		167.25		+ 1.50
	165.75	168.55/	170.45	Mar 20	164.85	− 2.80	
Mar 29	166.45				164.85		− 1.60
	166.45			May 3	173.35	+ 6.90	
May 15	177.70				173.35		− 4.35
	177.70	Jun	Sep	May 23	178.50	+ 0.80	
Jun 23	185.45	179.00/	181.00		178.50		− 4.95
	185.45			Jun 29	180.15	− 5.30	
Jul 10	184.45				180.15		− 4.30
	184.45			Aug 11	192.85	+ 8.40	
Aug 24	196.40				192.85		− 3.55
	196.40	Sep	Dec	Sep 6	194.25	− 2.15	
Sep 28	195.80	191.95/	194.20		194.25		+ 0.80
	195.80			Oct 31	189.75	− 6.05	
						+ 10.70	− 20.50
		− Commissions & Slippage				− 1.65	− 1.50
						+ 9.05	− 22.00

The biggest loss against an open position was on October 13 when the December 1989 NYFE contract closed at 180.90, down 14.90 from the position initiated on September 28 at 195.80. The biggest drawdown, which is the maximum amount lost in a series of losing closed-out trades, was $14.55 between May 23 and July 10. Such numbers are clearly unacceptable and it is certain that stops would have to be employed if the RSI were to be used alone. The $3 stop would have saved $5.35 on the long side and $6.20 on the short side. Since each dollar move is multiplied by 500, the use of such stops would improve performance considerably. However, I felt it important in designing a system using the RSL indicators to see how they performed on a stop and reverse basis.

2. MBI

The MBI might be expected to produce the same kind of results as the RSI. Interestingly, the MBI was better both on the long side and the short side, though the MBI suffered as did the RSI in not giving a sell signal until October 13. Interestingly, there were no profitable short signals during this period but the results still outperformed the RSI. Obviously, in the real world of futures trading, a trader can exit the market during the trading day and clearly does not have to wait for the day's closing price the way the mutual fund trader does; but in order to keep the playing field level, I stress that only close-only orders without stops were used so comparison between the indicators becomes possible.

The MBI as a stand-alone indicator gave the following results:

LONG		ROLLOVER		SHORT		PROFIT	
		Dec	Mar			Long	Short
Nov 22	151.20	154.15/	155.95	Jan 20	162.20	+ 9.20	
Mar 3	164.05	Mar	Jun		162.20		− 1.85
	164.05	168.55/	170.45	Mar 20	164.85	− 1.10	
Apr 3	168.15				164.85		− 3.30
	168.15			May 3	173.35	+ 5.20	
May 12	176.55				173.35		− 3.20
	176.55	Jun	Sep	Jun 12	182.40	+ 5.85	
Jun 26	184.75	179.00/	181.00		182.40		− 0.35
	184.75			Aug 11	192.85	+ 8.10	
Aug 25	195.75	Sep	Dec		192.85		− 2.90
	195.75	191.95/	194.20	Oct 25	190.30	− 7.70	
						+19.55	−11.60
		−Commissions & Slippage				− 1.20	− 1.05
						+18.35	−12.65

The maximum move against an open position was similar to that of the RSI but the maximum drawdown during this period was less, namely, $6.25. Trading only from the long side, the MBI would have been quite successful. It is obvious that the MBI should not be used for trading the short side *in this time period*, as the market trend was basically up and the MBI, as we have already noted, tends to top out ahead of the market.

3. **W(D)^{10}**

Attention has already been paid to the profitability of this indicator. The only problem with it is that it does not always follow market declines. During this period, the signal gave one superb buy and a sell short followed by a cover short, not go long signal on a trendline break. The results were as follows:

LONG		ROLLOVER		SHORT		PROFIT	
		Dec	Mar			Long	Short
Nov 21	150.50	154/15	155.95	Feb 9	167.25	+ 14.95	
Mar 3	164.05				167.25		+ 3.20
						+ 14.95	+ 3.20
		— Commissions & Slippage				− 0.30	− 0.15
						+ 14.65	+ 3.06

The W(D)^{10} did not trigger after March 3 so this clearly cannot be used as a stand alone indicator by anyone except a very patient trader. Once you are in a trade, however, the indicator characteristically keeps you in for a significant time. For the trade initiated on March 21 at 150.50, the maximum amount of movement against this entry figure was 1.10 (149.40 was the intraday low of 11/25/88). Once the position developed a profit, there were no significant moves against the position (See futures tables).

163

4. 0.1 A/D

In past years, this indicator has performed very well in mutual fund trading; but like all moving average indicators, it goes through periods when it whipsaws badly. Though it is useful as part of the RSL System for mutual funds, it became clear after analyzing its results as a stand-alone indicator for futures that too many signals and too many whipsaws occurred during this period for the indicator to be useful for futures trading. There were thirty round-trip signals during the test period with small losses (− 1.25 long and − 0.15 short) *before* commissions and slippage. This indicator, therefore, was dropped from consideration for futures trading.

5. The 21/5

This indicator allows the mutual fund trader to stay in some quite significant moves against a mutual fund position (Figure 29). It tends to trigger when the RSI is in midrange. Analysis of the indicator as a stand-alone indicator during the test period showed gains (after commissions and slippage) of $3.35 on the long side and losses of $12.00 on the short side. I felt that this indicator, while of definite value for mutual fund trading, did not add anything of significance to a system designed for futures and options trading because of the lag time involved in receiving the signals (as with all moving average systems). So, this indicator was also dropped.

6. The SW Envelope Indicator

We have seen how valuable this indicator is in trading mutual funds, particularly for entry signals. Analyzing the time period under study, it gave 36 round trip signals—even more than the 0.1 A/D. Very importantly, however, the long signals showed a profit after commissions and slippage of $25.35. The short side showed a loss of $3.70 (after commissions and slippage). This indicator can clearly be incorporated into a futures trading system based on the RSL indicators that pass the stand-alone test.

7. The DW Envelope Indicator

This indicator triggers after the SW Envelope Indicator. Occasionally, they will both trigger together. But, the DW can never trigger before the SW. During the test period, this indicator gave the following signals:

LONG		ROLLOVER		SHORT		PROFIT	
		Dec	Mar			Long	Short
Nov 28	151.45	154.15/	155.95	Feb 10	164.80	+ 11.55	
Mar 3	164.05				164.80		+ 0.75
	164.05	Mar	Jun	Mar 16	168.55	+ 4.50	
Mar 28	165.75	168.55/	170.45		170.45		+ 4.70
	165.75	Jun	Sep	Jun 15	179.00	+ 13.25	
Jul 10	184.45	179.00/	181.00		181.00		− 3.45
	184.45			Aug 14	192.40	+ 7.95	
Aug 24	196.40				192.40		− 4.00
	196.40	Sep	Dec	Sep 6	194.25	− 2.15	
Sep 28	195.80	191.95/	194.20		194.25		+ 0.70
	195.80			Oct 13	180.90	− 14.90	
						+ 20.20	− 1.30
		− Commissions & Slippage				− 1.05	− 1.20
						+ 19.15·	− 2.50

The violent down day, Friday October 13, triggered the indicator which up to that point had performed very well on the long side. In keeping with the concept of using close-only trades, the position took a loss of $14.90, obviously far too great a loss to sustain in actual trading. There were some moves of some significance against open positions. For instance, the June 15 short sale, closed out July 10, had an intrady high of − $5.75 against the position. In futures trading, moves of such magnitude are uncomfortable and should be avoided by using stops. We will examine stops further when we put the trading indicators together. Note that of the indicators discussed so far, only the $W(D)^{10}$ has shown a profit on the short side and that indicator only generated one short trade.

8. The NAT Indicator

This combined indicator is useful in mutual fund trading and gave a great signal before the October 1987 crash (Figure 25). The following signals were obtained during the test period.

LONG		ROLLOVER		SHORT		PROFIT	
						Long	Short
		Dec	Mar				
Nov 28	151.45	154.15/	155.95	Feb 9	167.25	+14.00	
		Mar	Jun				
Apr 13	167.95	168.55/	170.55		167.25		+1.30
	167.95			May 4	173.25	+ 5.30	
May 12	176.55	Jun	Sep		173.25		−3.30
	176.55	179.00/	181.00	Jun 30	179.10	+ 0.55	
Jul 13	186.00				179.10		−6.90
	186.00			Aug 21	189.95	+ 3.95	
Aug 24	196.40				189.95		−6.45
	196.40	Sep	Dec	Sep 7	193.50	− 2.90	
Sep 28	195.80	191.95/	194.20		193.50		−0.05
	195.80			Oct 12	198.90	+ 3.10	
Oct 31	189.75				198.90		+9.15
						+24.00	− 6.25
			− Commissions & Slippage			− 1.20	− 1.35
						+22.80	− 7.60

This indicator also did not profit on the short side under the conditions of the test; however, the long side trades were excellent.

166

PUTTING A SYSTEM TOGETHER

From analyzing the results of the performance of the individual RSL indicators, some conclusions may be drawn:

1. The market was basically in an uptrend during this time period.

2. All indicators were significantly more accurate for long positions than they were on the short side.

3. Only the $W(D)^{10}$ gave a profitable short sale overall performance. But there was only one signal.

4. In view of these findings and the market climate, only long signals will be taken during this time period for performance assessment.

5. Short sell signals will be kept and attention paid to them, as it is clear that in a bear market the short side signals will outperform the long side signals.

6. The RSL and MBI will be counted as *one* indicator.

7. The 0.1 A/D and the 21/5 will be dropped.

8. This leaves five basic indicators:

   RSI or MBI
   $W(D)^{10}$
   SW Envelope
   DW Envelope
   NAT

9. Long positions will be taken when two of the five indicators turn positive. The SW Envelope Indicator will be used as an initiating long side indicator only. Sell signals will be generated when two out of the other four indicators turn negative.

10. Though no short sales will be undertaken (because of the market climate and indicator performance), all sell signals will be closely monitored for potential profit and a possible shift in market climate.

11. A $3.00 stop will be placed at the time of the initial entry order and a $5.00 stop off the most recent closing high will be placed as soon as the position has developed a $3.00 profit.

The results are interesting for the following reasons:

RSL COMBINED RESULTS
(For Futures)

LONG		ROLLOVER		SELL		PROFIT/LOSS
		Dec	Mar			
Nov 21, '88	150.50	154.15/	155.95	Feb 9	167.25	+ 14.95
		Mar	Jun			
Mar 3, '89	164.05	168.55/	170.45	May 4	173.25	+ 7.30
May 12	176.55			Jun 15	179.00	+ 2.45
Jul 10	184.45			Aug 14	192.40	+ 7.95
Aug 24	196.40			Sep 6	194.25	− 2.15
Sep 28	195.89			Oct 13	192.80	− 3.00
						+ 27.50
		− Commissions & Slippage				− 1.20
						+ 26.30

1. The Combined RSL Indicators outperformed any of the individual indicators.

2. Only one of the stops was hit.

3. This was on October 13. The day did not start off as a slam dunk so it is possible that a price close to our stop could have been obtained. But even a $1.00 slippage would still have resulted in creditable performance. Indeed, if starting with a $10,000 stake, the signals would have generated a profit of $13,150 or 131.5%, and these were close only signals using the selected RSL Indicators.

4. Never neglect the short side. The market during this test period was uptrended and the short sale signals were not successful. But exactly the same thing happens to the long signals when the bear reigns. Then all the short signals clean up. *Be flexible.* During this period, to be long was to be king. But time periods change and so should one's thinking.

The trading plan is to wait for the market to come to you. It is very tempting to want to go out and "crush" the market into yielding a profit. But the successful trader waits until the tumblers are in place. In our case, we want the RSI *or* MBI to have given a buy and we need one of the other indicators to trigger. The plan in this market climate is to go long on the close, and to stay long until an RSL market sell *is* received or the $3.00 stop is hit. I really do not like money management stops—as I have discussed—believing market stops are far preferable. The trouble with trading futures is that the market stop may be too far away from the position for comfort. Perhaps that is the trade to avoid. The decision is up to the individual trader.

The results for the combined RSL Futures System would have been obtained by anyone following the RSL System, as they were taken on a close-only basis on a group of indicators that don't fool around. If the indicators trigger—that's it. They have done their job. I like to take positions in oversold territory *when I have some indication that the market is turning* (remember October 1987). It is quite frustrating in an ongoing bull market to be on the sidelines waiting for the correction that never wants to come. Using the RSL System for mutual funds, this is not a big problem as not all units will have been taken off the table. But with the RSL System for Futures, which is a one-contract, all-or-none system , how is such a period handled?

Fortunately, in the RSL System For Futures, we use the SW Envelope Indicator for opening positions only. This prevents some costly whipsaws. The idea is to stay with the trend as long as possible.

But how is the trend recognized?

The best indicator I know of for identifying the trend is, strange to relate, the Trend Indicator. Or rather, it is the point and figure specialized subindicator that I have come to rely on. This indicator will not only pick up trending markets but also trading range markets.

This indicator went on a buy on February 26, 1988 using standard point and figure technique. A major trendline is drawn at 45° from the reversal low (Figure 31). The major trend is assumed to be in effect until this line is broken. The indicator gave another buy signal on April 11, 1988 going into a trading range until early June 1988. The original signal of February 26, 1988 is still in effect as of November 23, 1989. Additional buy signals were given on October 6, 1988, January 9, 1989, April 3, 1989, and May 7, 1989. The TI reading as of November 23, 1989 is 3085, down from the high of October, 1989 of 3113.

But the major trendline is still intact and the TI would have to decline to 3065 to signal a point and figure sell. This sell would be a signal within an intact major trendline. So the major trend of the market is still assumed to be up in spite of the nonsense caused by program trading on October 13, 1989.

Ideally, a trending market should be followed until its RSL exit signal. This is more easily said than done, as there are times when the profit already achieved will make staying with the position quite difficult. So take some profit. It is a fabulous feeling to take the one you love out to dinner knowing you have won the money and then some. Just be careful though. Things can go wrong awfully quickly in the futures markets. I do not like stops as an initial protection against a significant loss *on a money management basis.* But I like them quite well, thank you, in their role of protecting a profit.

What about trading markets?

First off, trading markets are much more difficult for all market players than trending markets and are more difficult to recognize early on. When the stock market blasts off, which it likes to do in January, and then keeps on going, even an inexperienced market technician has little difficulty recognizing what is happening. But trading markets, by definition, require a trading range, and that means a good deal of backing and filling to establish the range.

The ideal play in trading markets involves the sale of options at the upper and lower boundaries of the trading range. We will be discussing options shortly. As far as the RSL System for Futures

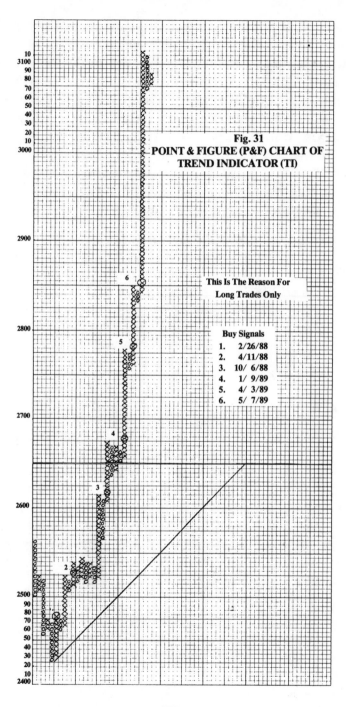

Fig. 31
POINT & FIGURE (P&F) CHART OF
TREND INDICATOR (TI)

This Is The Reason For
Long Trades Only

Buy Signals
1.   2/26/88
2.   4/11/88
3.   10/ 6/88
4.   1/ 9/89
5.   4/ 3/89
6.   5/ 7/89

171

is concerned, the best advice is to take the signals as they occur and then examine the profit/loss parameters. You will quickly realize the nature of the market you are in. When previously unprofitable (and avoided) short signals begin to become profitable, start thinking bear. This is the time to put out some short sales. We have seen how such trades should be avoided in a bull market, but I regret to report that I believe a big bear is waiting in the wings in the not too distant future. Short sales at RSL sell signals in such a market will not only buy you and the one you love a great dinner with caviar and Dom Perignon but at least a down payment on the restaurant itself.

NYFE CONTRACTS

(Note: Dec 89 given from 89 06 16—
Rollover Occurred 89 09 13)

File — 8:NFZ88R —   **Dec 88**

85:	881110	—	154.45	—	154.10	—	154.40
86:	881111	—	153.60	—	150.85	—	151.05
87:	881114	—	151.80	—	150.40	—	151.40
88:	881115	-	151.90	—	151.10	—	151.65
89:	881116	—	151.40	—	148.45	—	149.35
90:	881117	—	150.30	—	148.50	—	149.20
91:	881118	—	150.30	—	149.40	—	149.65
92:	881121	—	150.60	—	148.75	—	150.50
93:	881122	—	151.65	—	149.70	—	151.20
94:	881123	—	152.05	—	151.15	—	151.55
95:	881125	—	150.70	—	149.40	—	150.50
96:	881128	—	152.00	—	150.40	—	151.45
97:	881129	—	153.00	—	151.05	—	152.70
98:	881130	—	154.90	→	152.60	—	153.65
99:	881201	—	154.10	—	153.35	—	153.75
100:	881202	—	153.50	—	152.50	—	153.30
101:	881205	—	155.50	—	153.45	—	154.95
102:	881206	—	157.05	—	154.40	—	157.00
103:	881207	—	157.25	—	156.25	—	156.40
104:	881208	—	156.65	—	155.65	—	156.15
105:	881209	—	156.35	—	155.70	—	155.85
106:	881212	—	157.00	—	155.05	—	154.95
107:	881213	—	155.25	—	154.15	—	155.25
108:	881214	—	155.15	—	154.00	—	154.55
109:	881215	—	154.90	—	153.70	—	154.15

```
File - B:NFH89R -                                    Mar 89

 63: 881215   -   156.70   -   155.45   -   155.95
 64: 881216   -   157.25   -   156.10   -   156.75
 65: 881219   -   159.00   -   156.80   -   158.45
 66: 881220   -   159.75   -   157.40   -   157.85
 67: 881221   -   158.00   -   156.85   -   157.65
 68: 881222   -   157.95   -   157.20   -   157.25
 69: 881223   -   157.80   -   157.45   -   157.55
 70: 881227   -   157.75   -   156.95   -   157.20
 71: 881228   -   157.60   -   156.55   -   157.50
 72: 881229   -   158.85   -   157.55   -   158.45
 73: 881230   -   158.70   -   157.45   -   157.60
 74: 890103   -   156.95   -   155.00   -   156.00
 75: 890104   -   159.25   -   156.15   -   159.15
 76: 890105   -   160.15   -   158.55   -   159.15
 77: 890106   -   160.45   -   159.15   -   159.35
 78: 890109   -   160.15   -   158.85   -   159.50
 79: 890110   -   160.00   -   158.35   -   159.25
 80: 890111   -   160.25   -   158.65   -   160.00
 81: 890112   -   161.65   -   159.80   -   160.45
 82: 890113   -   161.15   -   160.05   -   160.85
 83: 890116   -   161.60   -   160.60   -   161.20
 84: 890117   -   161.10   -   160.30   -   160.75
 85: 890118   -   162.65   -   159.75   -   162.25
 86: 890119   -   162.95   -   161.75   -   162.65
 87: 890120   -   162.60   -   161.55   -   162.20
 88: 890123   -   163.15   -   160.65   -   161.00
 89: 890124   -   163.80   -   161.00   -   163.25
 90: 890125   -   163.65   -   162.55   -   163.60
 91: 890126   -   165.55   -   162.80   -   165.05
 92: 890127   -   167.60   -   165.30   -   166.35
 93: 890130   -   166.90   -   165.95   -   166.55
 94: 890131   -   168.15   -   165.65   -   167.60
 95: 890201   -   168.45   -   166.75   -   167.65
 96: 890202   -   168.15   -   166.60   -   167.25
 97: 890203   -   168.00   -   166.75   -   167.55
 98: 890206   -   167.85   -   166.30   -   166.95
 99: 890207   -   169.30   -   166.80   -   169.05
100: 890208   -   169.65   -   168.30   -   168.60
101: 890209   -   168.80   -   167.10   -   167.25
```

```
102:  890210  -  166.70  -  164.45  -  164.80
103:  890213  -  165.35  -  164.20  -  165.15
104:  890214  -  166.00  -  164.30  -  164.65
105:  890215  -  166.20  -  164.40  -  166.15
106:  890216  -  166.55  -  165.65  -  166.15
107:  890217  -  167.55  -  165.90  -  167.00
108:  890221  -  167.30  -  166.00  -  166.80
109:  890222  -  166.35  -  163.55  -  163.75
110:  890223  -  164.65  -  163.05  -  164.50
111:  890224  -  164.60  -  161.40  -  161.50
112:  890227  -  162.55  -  161.20  -  162.40
113:  890228  -  163.20  -  162.00  -  162.80
114:  890301  -  163.90  -  161.20  -  161.85
115:  890302  -  164.05  -  161.70  -  163.50
116:  890303  -  164.20  -  163.00  -  164.05
117:  890306  -  166.25  -  164.25  -  165.95
118:  890307  -  166.45  -  165.20  -  165.75
119:  890308  -  166.70  -  165.15  -  165.95
120:  890309  -  166.25  -  165.45  -  165.75
121:  890310  -  165.50  -  163.90  -  165.45
122:  890313  -  167.10  -  165.30  -  166.55
123:  890314  -  167.15  -  165.90  -  166.10
124:  890315  -  167.30  -  166.15  -  167.30
125:  890316  -  168.90  -  167.25  -  168.55
```

```
File - B:NFM89R -
```
Jun 89

```
61:  890316  -  171.05  -  169.20  -  170.45
62:  890317  -  167.00  -  163.45  -  165.95
63:  890320  -  165.90  -  163.95  -  164.85
64:  890321  -  166.20  -  165.10  -  165.65
65:  890322  -  165.85  -  164.75  -  165.40
66:  890323  -  166.05  -  163.80  -  164.25
67:  890327  -  165.55  -  163.45  -  165.20
68:  890328  -  166.35  -  165.30  -  165.75
69:  890329  -  166.50  -  165.35  -  166.45
70:  890330  -  167.20  -  165.45  -  166.10
71:  890331  -  167.80  -  166.35  -  167.35
```

72:	890403	—	168.90	—	167.20		168.15
73:	890404	—	168.40	—	167.35	—	168.25
74:	890405	—	168.55	—	167.70	—	168.15
75:	890406	—	167.80	—	167.05	—	167.55
76:	890407	—	169.30	—	165.85	—	168.95
77:	890410	—	169.35	—	168.35	—	168.60
78:	890411	—	169.70	—	168.60	—	169.65
79:	890412	—	170.30	—	169.40	—	169.55
80:	890413	—	169.20	—	167.55	—	167.95
81:	890414	—	170.80	—	169.30	—	170.65
82:	890417	—	171.15	—	170.35	—	170.95
83:	890418	—	173.40	—	172.20	—	172.85
84:	890419	—	173.90	—	172.50	—	173.40
85:	890420	—	174.05	—	171.75	—	173.50
86:	890421	—	174.55	—	173.35	—	174.45
87:	890425	—	174.80	—	172.90	—	173.00
88:	890426	—	173.55	—	172.45	—	173.05
89:	890427	—	175.30	—	173.15	—	174.50
90:	890428	—	174.75	—	173.95	—	174.40
91:	890501	—	174.40	—	173.15	—	174.35
92:	890502	—	174.95	—	173.00	—	173.10
93:	890503	—	173.75	—	172.65	—	173.35
94:	890504	—	173.45	—	172.55	—	173.25
95:	890505	—	174.80	—	172.15	—	172.25
96:	890508	—	172.50	—	171.20	—	172.45
97:	890509	—	172.80	—	170.85	—	171.65
98:	890510	—	172.40	—	171.15	—	171.95
99:	890511	—	172.95	—	171.85	—	172.70
100:	890512	—	176.60	—	174.70	—	176.55
101:	890515	—	177.75	—	175.45	—	177.70
102:	890516	—	177.50	—	176.85	—	177.10
103:	890517	—	178.50	—	176.75	—	178.10
104:	890518	—	178.85	—	177.60	—	178.60
105:	890519	—	180.25	—	178.95	—	179.90
106:	890522	—	181.05	—	179.20	—	180.25
107:	890523	—	179.90	—	178.35	—	178.50
108:	890524	—	178.95	—	177.80	—	178.65
109:	890525	—	179.25	—	178.10	—	178.90
110:	890526	—	180.00	—	178.75	—	179.80
111:	890530	—	180.45	—	177.50	—	178.35
112:	890531	—	179.95	—	178.15	—	179.15
113:	890601	—	180.55	—	178.70	—	179.85

```
114: 890602  -  182.25  -  180.85  -  182.00
115: 890605  -  182.25  -  179.75  -  180.05
116: 890606  -  181.50  -  179.35  -  181.20
117: 890607  -  183.20  -  181.60  -  182.65
118: 890608  -  183.10  -  181.90  -  183.00
119: 890609  -  183.40  -  181.60  -  182.80
120: 890612  -  182.55  -  180.85  -  182.40
121: 890613  -  181.90  -  180.40  -  180.90
122: 890614  -  181.40  -  180.20  -  180.90
123: 890615  -  180.65  -  178.35  -  179.00
```

```
File — B:NFU89R —
```
Sep 89

```
62: 890615  -  183.15  -  180.30  -  181.00
63: 890616  -  182.00  -  180.00  -  181.85
64: 890619  -  182.35  -  181.30  -  182.05
65: 890620  -  182.85  -  181.35  -  181.75
66: 890621  -  182.25  -  180.35  -  181.20
67: 890622  -  182.70  -  181.05  -  182.65
68: 890623  -  185.60  -  183.25  -  185.45
69: 890626  -  185.75  -  184.35  -  184.75
70: 890627  -  186.25  -  184.95  -  185.75
71: 890628  -  185.25  -  183.05  -  183.85
72: 890629  -  183.45  -  180.00  -  180.15
73: 890630  -  180.50  -  177.35  -  179.10
74: 890703  -  179.90  -  178.65  -  178.51
75: 890705  -  181.60  -  178.55  -  181.00
76: 890706  -  181.50  -  180.40  -  181.10
77: 890707  -  184.10  -  180.70  -  183.35
78: 890710  -  184.50  -  183.20  -  184.45
79: 890711  -  186.60  -  184.75  -  184.95
80: 890712  -  186.40  -  184.55  -  186.15
81: 890713  -  186.50  -  185.30  -  186.00
82: 890714  -  187.30  -  183.95  -  187.15
83: 890717  -  187.70  -  186.15  -  187.10
84: 890718  -  186.85  -  185.80  -  186.65
85: 890719  -  189.00  -  187.05  -  188.70
86: 890720  -  189.90  -  187.00  -  187.45
87: 890721  -  188.50  -  186.40  -  188.35
88: 890724  -  188.40  -  186.95  -  187.35
```

```
 89:  890725  —  189.00  —  186.50  —  187.35
 90:  890726  —  190.05  —  186.75  —  189.85
 91:  890727  —  192.10  —  190.15  —  191.85
 92:  890728  —  192.35  —  191.30  —  191.65
 93:  890731  —  194.00  —  191.45  —  193.90
 94:  890801  —  195.15  —  191.60  —  191.75
 95:  890802  —  193.50  —  191.40  —  193.40
 96:  890803  —  193.65  —  192.50  —  193.15
 97:  890804  —  193.80  —  191.50  —  192.60
 98:  890807  —  195.75  —  192.55  —  195.55
 99:  890808  —  195.80  —  194.70  —  195.20
100:  890809  —  196.40  —  193.75  —  193.85
101:  890810  —  196.00  —  193.00  —  194.75
102:  890811  —  196.70  —  192.20  —  192.85
103:  890814  —  193.75  —  191.25  —  192.40
104:  890815  —  193.55  —  192.00  —  193.40
105:  890816  —  194.20  —  193.05  —  193.20
106:  890817  —  194.05  —  191.70  —  192.90
107:  890818  —  193.75  —  192.45  —  193.70
108:  890821  —  193.90  —  189.90  —  189.95
109:  890822  —  191.15  —  189.30  —  191.10
110:  890823  —  193.10  —  190.65  —  193.00
111:  890824  —  196.55  —  193.10  —  196.40
112:  890825  —  197.05  —  194.90  —  195.75
113:  890828  —  196.25  —  194.50  —  196.15
114:  890829  —  196.25  —  194.30  —  194.75
115:  890830  —  196.55  —  194.00  —  195.60
116:  890831  —  196.10  —  195.10  —  195.50
117:  890901  —  197.40  —  195.35  —  196.55
118:  890905  —  197.30  —  195.50  —  196.20
119:  890906  —  195.85  —  193.60  —  194.25
120:  890907  —  195.00  —  193.40  —  193.50
121:  890908  —  194.75  —  192.00  —  193.95
122:  890911  —  193.90  —  192.40  —  193.80
123:  890912  —  194.50  —  193.50  —  193.90
124:  890913  —  194.65  —  191.50  —  191.95
```

```
File - B:NFZ89R -
```
Dec 89

```
 1: 890616  -  184.00  -  183.05  -  184.00
 2: 890619  -  184.15  -  183.90  -  184.20
 3: 890620  -  184.85  -  184.20  -  183.90
 4: 890621  -  184.30  -  182.80  -  183.35
 5: 890622  -  185.20  -  183.45  -  184.85
 6: 890623  -  187.70  -  185.65  -  187.70
 7: 890626  -  187.80  -  187.40  -  187.00
 8: 890627  -  188.10  -  187.40  -  188.00
 9: 890628  -  187.25  -  185.40  -  186.10
10: 890629  -  185.35  -  182.20  -  182.30
11: 890630  -  181.90  -  179.50  -  181.25
12: 890703  -  181.85  -  181.25  -  181.90
13: 890705  -  183.40  -  180.90  -  183.10
14: 890706  -  183.50  -  182.80  -  183.20
15: 890707  -  185.90  -  183.10  -  185.45
16: 890710  -  186.65  -  185.40  -  186.55
17: 890711  -  188.60  -  187.05  -  187.00
18: 890712  -  188.50  -  187.00  -  188.20
19: 890713  -  188.40  -  187.65  -  188.05
20: 890714  -  189.35  -  185.90  -  189.25
21: 890717  -  189.60  -  188.60  -  189.30
22: 890718  -  188.90  -  188.15  -  188.80
23: 890719  -  191.05  -  189.40  -  190.95
24: 890720  -  191.85  -  189.20  -  189.60
25: 890721  -  190.55  -  189.10  -  190.55
26: 890724  -  190.50  -  189.10  -  189.50
27: 890725  -  191.10  -  188.80  -  189.55
28: 890726  -  192.20  -  189.15  -  192.05
29: 890727  -  194.15  -  192.45  -  194.05
30: 890728  -  194.50  -  193.50  -  193.85
31: 890731  -  196.15  -  193.60  -  196.10
32: 890801  -  197.30  -  193.40  -  193.95
33: 890802  -  195.60  -  193.95  -  195.55
34: 890803  -  195.80  -  194.80  -  195.35
35: 890804  -  195.90  -  193.90  -  194.75
36: 890807  -  198.00  -  194.90  -  197.75
37: 890808  -  198.15  -  197.20  -  197.45
38: 890809  -  198.65  -  196.10  -  196.15
39: 890810  -  198.20  -  195.50  -  196.90
```

178

40:	890811	—	198.85	—	194.30	—	195.10
41:	890814	—	196.05	—	193.50	—	194.70
42:	890815	—	195.65	—	194.55	—	195.70
43:	890816	—	196.40	—	195.50	—	195.50
44:	890817	—	196.15	—	194.30	—	195.15
45:	890818	—	196.05	—	194.80	—	196.00
46:	890821	—	196.10	—	192.20	—	192.25
47:	890822	—	193.50	—	191.70	—	193.40
48:	890823	—	195.40	—	193.00	—	195.30
49:	890824	—	198.90	—	195.35	—	198.75
50:	890825	—	199.30	—	197.35	—	198.15
51:	890828	—	198.65	—	196.95	—	198.55
52:	890829	—	198.60	—	196.70	—	197.20
53:	890830	—	198.95	—	196.35	—	198.00
54:	890831	—	198.45	—	197.50	—	197.95
55:	890901	—	199.80	—	197.90	—	199.05
56:	890905	—	199.70	—	198.00	—	198.70
57:	890906	—	198.30	—	196.15	—	196.80
58:	890907	—	197.55	—	195.90	—	195.95
59:	890908	—	197.20	—	194.55	—	196.35
60:	890911	—	196.50	—	194.75	—	196.25
61:	890912	—	197.00	—	196.00	—	196.45
62:	890913	—	197.40	—	193.90	—	194.20
63:	890914	—	194.65	—	192.90	—	193.50
64:	890915	—	194.40	—	191.95	—	194.25
65:	890918	—	195.55	—	193.80	—	195.35
66:	890919	—	196.00	—	194.75	—	194.90
67:	890920	—	195.50	—	194.45	—	195.40
68:	890921	—	196.30	—	193.80	—	194.45
69:	890922	—	195.40	—	194.20	—	195.05
70:	890925	—	194.70	—	192.85	—	193.55
71:	890926	—	195.20	—	193.70	—	194.40
72:	890927	—	194.45	—	192.60	—	194.35
73:	890928	—	196.00	—	194.05	—	195.80
74:	890929	—	197.00	—	195.35	—	195.85
75:	891002	—	197.35	—	195.45	—	197.20
76:	891003	—	199.50	—	197.40	—	199.45
77:	891004	—	200.75	—	199.10	—	200.35
78:	891005	—	200.65	—	199.65	—	200.40
79:	891006	—	201.15	—	200.10	—,	200.95
80:	891009	—	201.85	—	200.75	—	201.65

179

```
 81:  891010  —  201.95  —  200.45  —  201.25
 82:  891011  —  201.05  —  199.10  —  199.45
 83:  891012  —  199.70  —  198.55  —  198.90
 84:  891013  —  199.20  —  180.90  —  180.90
 85:  891016  —  191.60  —  176.00  —  190.70
 86:  891017  —  191.10  —  186.50  —  190.40
 87:  891018  —  191.80  —  188.70  —  190.75
 88:  891019  —  194.90  —  191.40  —  193.50
 89:  891020  —  193.95  —  191.65  —  193.90
 90:  891023  —  194.10  —  191.60  —  192.35
 91:  891024  —  192.25  —  185.35  —  191.80
 92:  891025  —  191.85  —  170.05  —  190.30
 93:  891026  —  190.40  —  187.10  —  187.70
 94:  891027  —  188.30  —  185.10  —  186.55
 95:  891030  —  187.85  —  185.70  —  186.60
 96:  891031  —  189.95  —  187.45  —  189.75
 97:  891101  —  190.30  —  188.80  —  189.85
 98:  891102  —  189.75  —  187.20  —  187.95
 99:  891103  —  189.45  —  187.10  —  188.05
100:  891106  —  187.30  —  184.75  —  184.90
101:  891107  —  187.00  —  184.20  —  186.55
102:  891108  —  189.35  —  186.85  —  188.40
103:  891109  —  189.00  —  187.05  —  187.35
104:  891110  —  189.20  —  187.90  —  189.05
105:  891113  —  189.80  —  187.85  —  189.40
106:  891114  —  189.70  —  187.45  —  188.20
```

Chapter 11

What Should One Do About Trading Options?

We have seen how only the long side signals generated profit during this testing period. When trading options, the course of action is simple. Sell puts at a strike at least two strikes below that of the current index at the time when the RSL Indicators say "Buy." Use a simple $1.00 stop loss and close out the position when the indicators go on sell. That is all there is to it in a bullish period. In a bearish market climate, the position is reversed. What one wants to do then is sell calls two strikes above the present strike price when the indicators go on "Sell." As always, however, what can be done about the fact that the RSL Indicators are more accurate on the buy side than on the sell side? Unfortunately, not much. It is a fact of life like death and taxes. The really important thing is to avoid taking long only positions in a bear market. I accept that most people would rather go long than short; indeed, only a small percentage of investors/traders have gone or regularly go short. I have no prejudice against either side of the playing field. It just so happens that the indicators I use and rely on are more accurate on the long side than they are on the short side.

The short sale of an option has a built-in advantage—the time premium which is received immediately. I do not believe in buying options, as everything has to fall into place for the trade to be successful; but selling them is different. Selling options demands a certain amount of intraday market watching. I believe in selling options on futures such as the NYFE. This can be done in a commodity account, the same account used for trading futures contracts. There are advantages to trading options on futures as opposed to options on the OEX (S&P 100). These are:

1. Options on commodity futures can be traded in a commodity account, not a separate brokerage account which is necessary for trading OEX options.
2. Commissions favor the commodity account.
3. Prices are quoted in decimals, which are much easier than the antiquated fractional system still used by the regular stock exchanges. (They allow program trading—why not decimals?) O.K., it doesn't take long to convert, but why should we have to?

The only disadvantage to trading options on futures as opposed to the OEX is liquidity. This can be quite a problem if the market gets on its high or low horse. However, the cushion in this type of trading is the two-strike edge. Although the market can gyrate wildly, the options don't do so as much.

I am most grateful to Mr. Jim Schmidt of *Timer Digest** for working out the profit/loss parameters for OEX puts sold at the buy signals received on the RSL Futures and Options System. They are given in the following table:

	TRADE DATE	OEX INDEX	SIGNAL	POSITION				PRICE	**PROFIT LOSS
Trade-1	11/21/88	252.80	Buy	Sold OEX	Jan	245 Puts		4.500	
Rolled	01/19/89	272.42	Close	Bot OEX	Jan	245 Puts		.063	+ $443.70
Forward	01/19/89		Buy	Sold OEX	Mar	265 Puts		3.875	
	02/09/89	285.05	Close	Bot OEX	Mar	265 Puts		1.063	+ $281.20
Trade-2	03/03/89	285.05	Buy	Sold OEX	Apr	270 Puts		4.000	
Rolled	04/20/89	287.86	Close	Bot OEX	Apr	270 Puts		.063	+ $393.70
Forward	04/20/89		Buy	Sold OEX	Jun	280 Puts		3.125	
	05/04/89	288.73	Close	Bot OEX	Jun	280 Puts		2.750	+ $ 37.50
Trade-3	05/12/89	286.67	Buy	Sold OEX	Jun	280 Puts		1.500	
	06/15/89	299.85	Close	Bot OEX	Jun	280 Puts		.063	+ $143.70
Trade-4	07/10/89	300.79	Buy	Sold OEX	Aug	295 Puts		3.750	
	08/14/89	319.90	Close	Bot OEX	Aug	295 Puts		0.063	+ $368.70
Trade-5	08/24/89	320.73	Buy	Sold OEX	Oct	315 Puts		4.250	
	09/06/89	328.51	Close	Bot OEX	Oct	315 Puts		2.563	+ $168.70
Trade-6	09/28/89	322.68	Buy	Sold OEX	Nov	315 Puts		3.500	
	10/13/89	330.76	Close	Bot OEX	Nov	315 Puts		5.500	+ $200.00

*Timer Digest, P.O. Box 1688, Greenwich
 CT 06836-1688

Total profit + $1,637.20

** Per Contract

It is important to realize that the OEX options trade at "times 100," so the profit and loss parameter should be multiplied by 5, as 5 puts would have been sold at each signal to match the futures performance (as futures trade at "times 500"). We have seen that buying futures would have yielded a profit of $26.30 times 500 equals $13,150.00. Selling 5 puts using the same signals would have yielded a profit of $8,186.00. It is, however, important to realize that this figure does not include commission costs or slippage.

The safest play is indeed to sell a put (or puts) in expectation of the market rise. Safest because the indicators are better on the long side than the short side. For the adventurous there is a play worth knowing about—the synthetic futures options position. On a buy signal, an out-of-the-money put is sold and an out-of-the-money call is bought. The trader here is expecting a pretty decent market advance.

When the market turns to bear—but only when the bear can be identified—the play is to sell a call above the market and buy a put below it. The options do not present such a pure play as the futures market, but they do offer a good deal of protection, certainly if strikes are sold away from the market. I don't think one should risk more than $1.00 under these situations. This, of course, translates into $500.00 on options on futures, and $500 on the OEX for five options. It is frustrating when the market comes down, triggers your stop, then turns right around, but the protection is usually worth it. In an uptrended period, it is better to avoid the short side of the market entirely. (Note that selling a put is a bullish strategy).

However, the short sell signals should be carefully monitored because as soon as they start showing some profit, it may mean that the trend of the market has changed. I have stressed in the main text the importance of playing both sides of the market; and when the next bear market hits, the short side will be clearly the side to be on.

Chapter 12

Putting It All Together

There are a number of indicators in the now-you-see-them, now-you-don't variety. I do not use them for market timing, but I mention them here without going into any great detail. These indicators are background music and should not be considered more important than that. But I should at least tell you what I have found to be useful over the years.

1. **The Interest Rate Picture.** *Investor's Daily* has a section giving charts of the following interest rates:
   (1) The Prime Rate: This is listed as the rate charged by banks on loans to the most credit-worthy corporations.
   (2) The Federal Funds Rate: This is the rate on overnight loans among financial institutions.
   (3) The Federal Reserve Board Discount Rate: This is the rate charged by the Federal Reserve on loans to commercial banks.
   (4) The three-month yield on Treasury Bills: These are traded on a discount basis. The three-month bills are the ones to watch. They are also known as the 90-day bills and the 13-week bills.

(5) The thirty-year Treasury Bond Yield.

(6) The ninety-day Certificate of Deposit (CD) Rates which are the rates paid by major banks on new certificates in blocks of $1,000,000 or more.

(7) The yield on Moody's Aa Utilities.

(8) The rates on tax exempt bonds. Also given is the yield curve, highlighting the difference between the length of time to maturity and the corresponding yield for U.S. Treasuries.

It is unnecessary to plot any of these indicators. They are readily attainable from Investor's Daily, which I consider an outstanding financial publication and essential for those trading the RSL System. Really, all you have to do is glance at the tables. If rates are going up, that is bad news for the market (other factors being equal). Note, however, that the market can mount a rally during a period of rising interest rates. If rates are declining, that is good news for the market. Market declines in such an environment are likely to be mild and short-lived. But, I would stress these interest rate figures are only background music.

2. **The Value of $1.00 Dividends on the DJIA.** Each week, Barron's publishes the dividends paid on the Dow Stocks and the effective yield. It is a simple matter to divide the closing value of the Dow by the dividends paid to find out what price investors are prepared to pay for $1.00 of dividends. When the figure gets up to (and certainly when it gets over) $30.00 per $1.00 of dividends, watch out. This is also not a *timing* indicator, as the market can stay up in this range for longer than expected. But ultimately it will fall, bringing the value of $1.00 dividends back into the historic range below $30.00. Similarly, when the value falls into the low 20s, and certainly if it falls below 20 for each dollar of dividends, be prepared to do some buying (but only if the RSL Indicators say so).

Also in Barron's, under the weekly bond statistics are details of the difference in yield between the highest grade corporate bonds and the yield of the DJIA stocks. This is expressed as a negative number, since the yield on the Dow is compared with that on bonds. When the difference reaches − 6% or greater (i.e., bonds yield 6% more than stocks) watch out as money will tend to leave the stock market for the bond market. Again, this is not a timing indicator as such, but it is good to have the data tucked away somewhere in your mind. Like everything else in the market, this condition will ultimately correct back to historic norms, which are below − 6%.

3. **The Money Market Maturity and Yield Indicator.** When the money market average maturity increases and the yield drops, this is bullish for the market, as market professionals believe that interest rates will fall. The weekly figures are to be found in Barron's and are supplied by Donoghue's Fund Report, Holliston, MA 01746. I invented this indicator some time ago and it is quite good. What I did was to run a 0.2 exponential moving average of the raw data both for maturity and yield. I would then derive figures from the raw data, dividing maturity by yield, and compare these figures for the corresponding 0.2 exponential values. Table 18 will give you the idea.

When the figure from the raw data exceeds that from the 0.2 exponential MA data, the market is on buy, and vice-versa of course. The market went on buy during the week of 4/17/89. This is clearly not a precise timing indicator, but it is good to note that this monetary indicator is confirming the move. In Table 18, the value in Column I, The Average Maturity, is divided by the value in Column III, the Average Yield, and placed above the yield data figure in Column III. The 0.2 exponential moving average of the average maturity in Column II is then divided by the 0.2 exponential MA value of the average yield in Column IV. This value is posted above the 0.2 exponential MA figure in Column IV. During the week of 4/17/89, the raw data figure (3.70) exceeded the 0.2 exponential moving average figure (3.57), generating a buy signal.

187

Table 18
MATURITY/YIELD MONETARY INDICATOR

1989	Av. Maturity (1)	0.2 Exponential MA (2)	Av. Yield (3)	0.2 Exponential MA (4)	
			3.46	4.19	
1.3	29.0	33.32	8.39	7.96	
			3.86	4.06	
	30.0	32.58	8.28	8.02	
			3.59	3.96	
	30.0	32.06	8.35	8.09	
			3.81	3.93	
	32.0	32.05	8.38	8.15	
			3.81	3.91	
	32.0	32.04	8.40	8.20	
			3.70	3.87	
2.6	31.0	31.83	8.37	8.23	
			3.67	3.83	
	31.0	31.66	8.44	8.27	
			3.64	3.79	
	31.0	31.53	8.52	8.32	
			3.58	3.73	
	31.0	31.42	8.65	8.42	
			3.54	3.69	
3.6	31.0	31.34	8.75	8.49	
			3.62	3.68	
	32.0	31.47	8.85	8.56	
			3.46	3.63	
	31.0	31.38	8.95	8.64	
			3.43	3.59	
	31.0	31.30	9.04	8.72	
			3.41	3.55	
4.3	31.0	31.24	9.08	8.79	
			3.50	3.54	
	32.0	31.39	9.14	8.86	
			3.70	3.57	Buy (3.70 > 3.57)
	34.0	31.91	9.19	8.93	
			3.70	3.60	
	34.0	32.33	9.19	8.98	
			3.72	3.62	
5.1	34.0	32.66	9.15	9.01	
			3.72	3.64	
	34.0	32.93	9.15	9.04	
			4.15	3.70	
	38.0	33.54	9.16	9.06	
			4.16	3.79	
	38.0	34.43	9.14	9.08	
			4.06	3.84	
	37.0	34.94	9.11	9.09	
			4.19	3.91	
6.5	38.0	35.55	9.08	9.09	
			4.36	4.00	
	39.0	36.24	8.94	9.06	
			4.39	4.07	
	39.0	36.79	8.89	9.03	
			4.39	4.14	
	39.0	37.23	8.89	9.00	
			4.29	4.17	
7.3	38.0	37.38	8.85	8.97	
			4.57	4.25	
	40.0	37.90	8.75	8.92	
			4.85	4.37	
	42.0	38.72	8.66	8.87	

Monetary and sentiment indicators tend to be late. This indicator missed all the upward movement from November 1988 when the Comp was around 150 until the time of the signal, when the NY Comp was around 170. It is still worth following for all that. As far as monetary indicators go, it is better than most. For instance, in Barron's on 1/23/89 an indicator was described utilizing the ratio of the six-month premium on put options compared with the six-month premium on call options (Stuart P. Kaye wrote the article). That indicator went on sell on 11/25/88 and still had not gone back on buy as of 6/23/89. The sell was at Dow 2073.68; the Dow was at 2531.87 as of 6/23/89. That indicator is clearly not worth keeping (and I no longer do so).

Indicators, as an aside, should only be kept as long as they are useful in generating decisions. It is easy to get into the habit of keeping an indicator simply because that indicator is one of the indicators you've always kept. My idea is to give the indicator six months or so; and if it doesn't work out, throw it down l'oubliette, that place the French use for anything to be forgotten. Never fall in love with your indicators (just as those who play individual stocks should never fall in love with their stocks). If the indicator isn't working over a decent time frame, scrap it.

One of the great things about the indicators—described in this book as the RSL Indicators—is that I have a solid data base going back over the years, as far back as 1972 for the MBI, for example. I think it is unlikely that any one of these indicators will die out on us. But the beauty of the system is that it really doesn't matter if one indicator goes on the blink, as there are others available; and if they all go on the blink, then it is clear that the market, as I have come to know it, will have changed in a radical way. That *can* happen; anything *can*. But I would much rather bet that the tried and true indicators presented in this book will continue to perform rather than that they won't. In the long run, the market clearly only takes three courses of action. It can (1) stay flat, which isn't exciting for anyone, (2) go up; this pleases the bulls and squeezes the bears. The rate at which it does so is of some importance, but the trend is clearly the determinant. or (3) it can go down. As night follows day, there will be inevitable down periods, particularly after protracted advances. The RSL System seeks to gather a significant portion of the profit available. It is a risk-adverse system and on a risk-adjusted basis shines. There is no doubt but that the high roller who can correctly identify the start of a good move, say using the $W(D)^{10}$ indicator, and who puts the whole bet down will do better than we will using our fold-in approach. But there is also no doubt that the RSL approach will expose the trader to much less risk and that over the years it has provided some very substantial profits at greatly reduced risk. I have been able to see this in my own retirement account, and in such an account, it is important to avoid risk as much as possible. Obviously, the more risk you are prepared to take, the more reward you should legitimately expect.

The RSL System will give the trader the opportunity of becoming fully invested if the market shows it is "for real" by sustaining its advance and moving the RSI (and MBI) indicators higher.

For a long time now, I have kept extensive market notebooks and believe that what has stuck over the years may be of interest. Market lessons are seldom learned all at once. It is unfortunate that a mistake will have to be repeated before it really sinks in. It is just like learning to play chess. But once a mistake is recognized, and that will usually be on its repetition, it is really important from that point on to try to avoid repeating that particular mistake in the future. There are hundreds of mistakes out there waiting to happen, but they are all related to a few basic mistakes. My most persistent mistake (as shown by subsequent market action) has been to sell too soon. It has been very difficult for me to give the market the benefit of the doubt when the most sensitive short-term indicators were flashing sell. The problem is that such indicators can just as easily go back on buy the next day.

Using the RSL System, the idea is not to move all the units in at once and also not to move them *out* all at once—unless something big triggers all the stops. Fortunately, I was safely on the sidelines before the October 1987 crash, as a significant number of the RSL indicators had gone on sell.

One of the mistakes I learned to correct quite early was the fear of re-entering the market after a premature exit. Now, as long as the indicators give me an identifiable reason to do so, I go. I have stressed before that you need to have a reason for taking market action; that is, you never should act on the conviction that the market should "do such and such." The charge to the trader is to keep the indicators, identify the signals, *and use them.* That is all that anyone can expect of your interaction with the market. As I have mentioned before, there are times when the trade feels so wrong that it is difficult to act. Indeed, I hold some serious internal conversations with myself in order to do so. The interesting thing is that these trades work out as well as, and indeed sometimes better than, those "picture-perfect" trades with which a good deal of mental comfort is possible.

The following excerpts are from my diaries. There is no order about these entries. Each stands alone. I hope some may prove useful, as I have tried to select those that I think may have value from the trading diaries I have kept since 1973. It was quite a task going through them. It was only after I started to do so that I realized how much I had written since I started on my quest for market expertise. These are general market aphorisms.

1. Winning takes determination, courage, thought, patience, honesty, and a *sense of detachment from the results.*
2. He who is afraid to make decisions or mistakes is afraid to succeed.
3. Never trade against the trend in anticipation of a trend change.
4. Be prepared to buy new highs and sell new lows.
5. Play the market as conservatively as possible relative to satisfactory gains.
6. The real test of the trader is to see if he can stay with a profitable position.
7. You have to accept that you cannot win on every roll.
8. Those who ride alone must sit tall in the saddle.
9. Never over-ride your indicators; never predict.

191

10. Discipline is the essential ingredient of success.
11. There is no point in keeping indicators unless you use them.
12. Nothing in the market ever happens exactly the same way twice.
13. Only go into the market when you can identify a reasonable *market action* stop.
14. Avoid taking a buy on a day that has taken out the previous day's low during the day's trading action.
15. Never second-guess the market by thinking you know where it is going.
16. Success is using what you know properly.
17. Don't be in a rush to sell a strong up move and never sell it short unless the trend has clearly turned.
18. The market will pay attention to fundamental news when it needs an excuse to do so.
19. It is impossible to derive a mechanical system that works in all markets.
20. Day trading futures without a computer is like waving a hand out the window trying to catch air currents.
21. In all trading, you have to define a comfortable time frame and a comfortable level of risk.
22. Never chase a losing bet.
23. Try to find out as early as possible what works for you as an individual and stick with it.
24. Never try to salvage a losing option position by setting up a spread directly.
25. The trend by definition has changed whenever a shorter term moving average turns through a longer term moving average. The trend change, however, may be too short to be useful.
26. Let your indicators make your decisions; keep your own thoughts and especially your ego out of the decision-making process.

27. Know exactly why you are doing what you are doing. There has to be an identified and identifiable reason for every trade; also, for *not* trading.

    It is very important not to relate a trading decision to one's overall ability and intelligence. The trade may not succeed, but that does not mean the trader is a failure. That is why a sense of detachment is so important (and so difficult to acquire). It is essential *not* to get elated if you are winning or despondent if you are losing. They are opposite sides of the same coin.

28. Everything is more difficult than it looks.

29. The lessons one has learned in the market will lose their precision unless revisited frequently in one's thoughts, just as a foreign language once learned will soon become forgotten unless practiced frequently. This is an absolute truth.

30. It is certain that Rome was *not* built in a day.

31. A good trader accepts that he doesn't know where the market is going. He follows his system and takes all the signals. The market is unforgiving and you can get decapitated just by looking away for a moment.

32. The satisfaction that trading provides is trading *exactly by the book*. The book can be your book or somebody else's. Your own, of course, is to be preferred. It is not the market that is the real opponent; it is oneself. Avoid allowing someone else to trade your account for you unless you can truly forget about the market on a daily basis.

33. Never say to yourself or someone else, "I should have done so-and-so." Examine why you didn't and resolve not to let the next opportunity slip.

34. The sense of power achieved if one manages to gain true intrapersonal discipline is awesome.

35. The market is one of the greatest games going. And be sure it is a game, the score being kept in dollars. Never take losses personally.

36. Don't trade if you feel emotionally upset.
37. Don't jump from system to system, as that runs the danger of you leaving a system just before it reaches a successful period.
38. Markets are always there; it is the players who change. Many get tapped out.
39. When in doubt, get out. Learn to get out quickly. Do not be afraid to re-enter quickly if the market warrants doing so.
40. Always back off from a mistake.
41. There are no good or bad trades, only those that win or lose.
42. You have to get over the fear of losing money.
43. Make sure you have enough trading capital. Being under-capitalized is an invitation for the market to do you in.
44. It is difficult to re-enter a strong market after a premature exit, but it has to be done.
45. The nesting envelope signal is invaluable.
46. Try to avoid taking a vacation or trading break when the DW envelope is uptrended.
47. The market very seldom obliges one's wishes.
48. Don't try to predict market behavior based on previous seasonal action.
49. Never try to recoup a loss by increasing the size of your bet.
50. You have to think about the market *every day*.
51. If the market fails to move as expected within three days of initiating a position, prepare to exit.
52. The groundhog has to emerge, but don't try to guess when.

In this book, I have recorded everything of importance I have learned about the market. Nothing that I now consider to be important has been withheld. The text is not long, but it does represent a great deal of time spent studying the market. I have thought about it, worried about it, and studied the market now for 20 years or so. This book presents the indicators that have worked the best for me. Over the years, I have kept scores of indicators and indeed invented several. Any indicator can work well for awhile. But I need a tried and true indicator with a good track record before trusting that indicator with my money. The indicators in the RSL System are so time tested that I can recommend them to you. I have tried to make this a practical book, one that can be used as soon as relative data are accumulated. Trading the markets, any market, is a struggle. The trader who has taken a position opposite to yours is betting that you will be wrong. This is not a game for those without the will to win.

I mentioned earlier the intelligent child. This concept is invaluable. As long as I can say to the intelligent child, "You see this. That is why I did what I did," then I have fulfilled all the criteria I demand of myself. I cannot demand perfection, as such is not possible in any endeavor. I cannot demand success, as that is a light that flicks on and off. But I can and do demand of myself a disciplined approach.

Although you will never meet the opponent on the other side of your trade, if you're trading options or futures, that trader is your foe. Either he wins or you do, it is that simple. (The house has the only sure thing as it collects commissions from both players). I used to trade futures contracts actively, but no longer do so as actively because of the stress and leverage involved. It is much easier on the nervous system to trade mutual funds using the RSL Indicators with the one problem of not being able to get out during a big down day. This problem does not apply to futures trading. When the stop is entered as a stop there is a good chance of being executed at a price reasonably close to that selected. I believe position trading in futures is the way to go. I was impressed that Stanley Kroll, a veteran futures trader, in his recent book, *Kroll on Futures Trading Strategy,*[8] obviously thought so too.

A position in one futures contract taken on the W(D)[10] buy signal on November 21, 1988 and held until the 10° trendline exit signal in February would have yielded a profit of approximately $7500.00 per contract. (The December contract would have had to have been rolled over). An equally spectacular gain would have been possible trading options. The real question, of course, that the trader has to face is the simple one: Could I have ridden with my profit to the conclusion of the signal?

I have always had difficulty giving the futures enough room, as I have a tendency to think in terms of the absolute profit or loss. If I lose $2000.00, that feels very much like a $2000.00 loss of real money. It is real, of course, but the $2000.00 we are talking about here is not to be confused with those same $2000.00 outside the market that goes to pay for all the essentials. You know what they are as well as I do. The only way I know to be a successful trader is to take a stake and mentally *kiss it good-bye*, by which I mean there should never be any liens on the money like education or rent. You have to say to yourself in effect:

1. I have this much discretionary income that I am going to use to trade the market either in futures or mutual funds. And if this money is lost in its entirety, it will not affect my life-style one iota.

2. I am going to use market stops. That is, stops based on the action of the market itself, not money management stops (see discussion under RSI stops).

It is, of course, the leverage that makes futures trading so attractive and so difficult. In my opinion, undercapitalization is the main problem futures traders face. I believe that you should have as a minimum $35,000 of equity for each S&P and $20,000 for each NYFE contract, to be able to use market stops. Leverage is what futures trading is all about. What would I advise a trader with $10,000 in discretionary income to do? I would have to give the following advice based on a good deal of experience.

1. Forget the futures markets, and in particular don't be tempted to join a futures commodity limited partnership. Returns may be worthwhile (though often they are not) but satisfaction comes from making your own decisions and having them work out.

2. O.K., so you still want to trade futures? Well, trade the safest and most successful signals you can find.

The W(D)^{10} signal is certainly worth considering, but you may have to wait a long time for signals to form.

3. Trade spreads such as the S&P/Value-Line spread discussed in Chapter 1.
4. Trade mutual funds using the RSL System and watch your modest profits grow. This is my preferred route and what the RSL System is all about. There are, of course, no guarantees that this system will continue to be successful, but it is certain that the risk involved is much less than in trading futures. Also, of course, the profits will be less if the trades are successful.

I have also mentioned that you should try to trade both sides of the market. This is easy to do in stocks, futures and options but the average open-ended mutual fund can only be traded from the long side. I do not recommend shorting closed-end mutual funds as already discussed, as they often trade at a discount to net asset value. So, the mutual fund trader really has to be long or in cash, which is not such a bad place to be when the market is falling. It is interesting when looking at the figures in the Hulbert Financial Digest to note that those newsletters with programs that recommend shorting in their portfolios really did not do that much better than those that do not recommend shorting. Indeed, in some cases, they did not do as well.

The idea of exploring both sides of the market is, I believe, best exploited by selling options. Such an endeavor demands exquisite market timing and the determination not to take a big hit. Although I do not do much option trading now, I did a good deal previously and, as mentioned, did well selling naked calls in the 1974 bear market.

I also believe that some very decent profits could be made by selling puts against stock that you wished to own at times when the RSL indicators were oversold and going on buy. A put option in effect allows you to buy a stock at a discount if it is "put" to you, or to pocket the premium if it is not. This strategy is inherently more dangerous, of course, than those involving the purchase of options. Anyone with a naked short put position learned this very forcefully in October 1987; but my contention is that there was no reason to sell or hold naked puts then, as all the RSL indicators were on sell. The RSL Indicators do not try to anticipate market change, only to pick up such change as soon as possible after it has occurred.

This, then, is the RSL System. It is a market timing system suitable for timing trades in mutual funds, futures, stocks, and options. It demands a certain amount of time and a good deal of discipline. But, importantly, it works—or perhaps, I should say that it has worked for me and that I see no reason whatsoever why it should not work for anyone else. Just remember:

1. Keep good worksheets and charts, and
2. Follow the signals.

That's all you have to do. But you have to have the courage to go when the indicators say so.

I hope I have been of help.

All the best.

Humphrey E.D. Lloyd

A Final Thought And A
Unique Feature Of This Book

Trading has to be fun as well as profitable. This book is for those traders wishing to profit from another trader's experience and so curtail the apprenticeship demanded of all market players. I have arranged with the publisher to supply accurate data to any purchaser of this book for the month immediately prior to purchase. Such data will be taken from my worksheets and updated on a monthly basis. And, it will be available within five days of the last trading day of the month.

This will enable any trader buying this book to get the indicators up and running far more quickly than could be possible if you were starting your initial data base from the date of purchase. Two data sheets will be provided with each book, at your request.

1. The MBI for the previous month.
   This will require a full data sheet on its own.
2. A monthly update of the following indicators: RSI, A/D + 0.2A/D, 21/5, and TI. Buy and sell signals for the SW and DW Envelope Indicators during the previous month will also be given (no math is involved in these indicators) as point-and-figure signals (if any) on the TI.

Good Trading

Bibliography

1. Wilder, J. Welles, Jr., 1978, *New Concepts in Technical Trading Systems,* available from Windsor Books, Brightwaters, NY, 11718.

2. *Stock Traders Almanac,* 1989, the Hirsch Organization, Six Deer Trail, Tappan, NJ 07675.

3. Colby, Robert W. and Meyers, Thomas A., 1988, *The Encyclopedia of Technical Market Indicators,* Dow Jones-Irwin, Homewood, IL 60430.

4. Williams, Larry R., 1972, *The Secret of Selecting Stocks for Immediate and Substantial Gains,* Windsor Books, Brightwaters, NY, 11718.

5. Lloyd, Humphrey E.D., 1976, *The Moving Balance System, A New Technique for Stock and Option Trading,* Windsor Books, Brightwaters, NY 11718.

6. Stewart, Joseph T., Jr., 1981, *Dynamic Stock Option Trading,* John Wiley and Sons, New York.

7. Hurst, J.M., 1970, *The Profit Magic of Stock Transaction Timing,* Prentice-Hall, Englewood Cliffs, NJ.

8. Kroll, Stanley, 1988, *Kroll on Futures Trading Strategy,* Dow Jones-Irwin, Homewood, IL 60430.